HIS NAME IS JESUS

Life and Power in the Master's Ministry

A Study of Matthew, Mark & Luke

Jack W. Hayford

with

Gary Matsdorf

THOMAS NELSON PUBLISHERS
Nashville • Atlanta • London • Vancouver

This, the third series of *Spirit-Filled Life
Bible Study Guides,* is dedicated to the
memory of

Dr. Roy H. Hicks, Jr.
(1944–1994)

one of God's "men for all seasons,"
faithful in the Word, mighty in the Spirit,
leading multitudes into the love of God
and the worship of His Son, Jesus Christ.

Unto Christ's glory and in Roy's memory,
we will continue to sing:

Praise the Name of Jesus,
Praise the Name of Jesus,
He's my Rock, He's my Fortress,
He's my Deliverer, in Him will I trust.
Praise the Name of Jesus.

Words by Roy Hicks, Jr. © 1976 Latter Rain Music. All rights administered by
The Sparrow Corporation. All rights reserved. Used by permission.

His Name is Jesus: Life and Power in the Master's Ministry
A Study of Matthew, Mark & Luke
© 1995 by Jack W. Hayford

Published in Nashville, Tennessee, by Thomas Nelson, Inc.

Printed in the United States of America
1 2 3 4 5 6 7 8 — 01 00 99 98 97 96 95

CONTENTS

About the Executive Editor

JACK W. HAYFORD, noted pastor, teacher, writer, and composer, is the Executive Editor of the complete series, working with the publisher in the conceiving and developing of each of the books.

Dr. Hayford is Senior Pastor of The Church On The Way, the First Foursquare Church of Van Nuys, California. He and his wife, Anna, have four married children, all of whom are active in either pastoral ministry or vital church life. As General Editor of the *Spirit-Filled Life Bible*, Pastor Hayford led a four-year project, which has resulted in the availability of one of today's most practical and popular study Bibles. He is author of more than twenty books, including *A Passion for Fullness, The Beauty of Spiritual Language, Rebuilding the Real You*, and *Prayer Is Invading the Impossible*. His musical compositions number over four hundred songs, including the widely sung "Majesty."

About the Writer

GARY MATSDORF is pastor of Faith Bible Center in Medford, Oregon, where he has served this growing congregation for more than eleven years. He is a graduate of Azusa Pacific University and Fuller Theological Seminary, and was also a member of the faculty of LIFE Bible College from 1975 to 1981.

Gary and his wife Velda have two teenage children, Travis and Tyler. Besides his pastoral duties, Gary is actively involved in missionary work in Jamaica and Spain. He also served as the Associate Editor of the *Spirit-Filled Life Bible*.

Of this contributor, the Executive Editor has remarked: "Few men have the gift of taking the deeper truths of God's Word and making them both practical and palatable for the average reader/student. Gary's commitment to personal integrity, in scholarship as well as in conduct, brings a unique quality of strength to his writing. I praise God for the kind of edification users of this guide will discover!"

THE GIFT
THAT KEEPS ON GIVING

One of the most precious gifts God has given us is His Word, the Bible. Wrapped in the glory and sacrifice of His Son and delivered by the power and ministry of His Spirit, it is a treasured gift—the gift that keeps on giving, because the Giver it reveals is inexhaustible in His love and grace.

Tragically, though, fewer and fewer people are opening this gift and seeking to understand what it's all about and how to use it. They often feel intimidated by it. It requires some assembly, and its instructions are hard to comprehend sometimes. How does the Bible fit together anyway? What does this ancient Book have to say to us who are looking toward the twenty-first century? Will taking the time and energy to understand its instructions and to fit it all together really help you and me?

Yes. Yes. Without a shred of doubt.

The *Spirit-Filled Life Bible Discovery Guide* series is designed to help you unwrap, assemble, and enjoy all God has for you in the pages of Scripture. It will focus your time and energy on the books of the Bible, the people and places they describe, and the themes and life applications that flow thick from its pages like honey oozing from a beehive.

So you can get the most out of God's Word, this series has a number of helpful features:

"WORD WEALTH" provides definitions of key terms.

"BEHIND THE SCENES" supplies information about cultural practices, doctrinal disputes, business trades, etc.

"AT A GLANCE" features helpful maps and charts.

"BIBLE EXTRA" will guide you to other resources that will enable you to glean more from the Bible's wealth.

"PROBING THE DEPTHS" will explain controversial issues raised by particular lessons and cite Bible passages and other sources to help you come to your own conclusions.

The "FAITH ALIVE" feature will help you see and apply the Bible to your day-to-day needs.

The only resources you need to complete and apply these study guides are a heart and mind open to the Holy Spirit, a prayerful attitude, and a pencil and a Bible. Of course, you may draw upon other sources, but these study guides are comprehensive enough to give you all you need to gain a good, basic understanding of the Bible book being covered and how you can apply its themes and counsel to your life.

A word of warning, though. By itself, Bible study will not transform your life. It will not give you power, peace, joy, comfort, hope, and a number of other gifts God longs for you to unwrap and enjoy. Through Bible study, you will grow in your understanding of the Lord, His kingdom and your place in it, but you must be sure to rely on the Holy Spirit to guide your study and your application of the Bible's truths. He, Jesus promised, was sent to teach us "all things" (John 14:26; cf. 1 Cor. 2:13). Bathe your study time in prayer, asking the Spirit of God to illuminate the text, enlighten your mind, humble your will, and comfort your heart. He will never let you down.

My prayer and goal for you is that as you unwrap and begin to explore God's Book for living His way, the Holy Spirit will fill every fiber of your being with the joy and power God longs to give all His children. So read on. Be diligent. Stay open and submissive to Him. You will not be disappointed. He promises you!

Lesson 1/Jesus Christ, the Son of David, the Son of God

Have you ever watched a masterful attorney in the courtroom? Often he will parade before the jury a number of witnesses, all of whom credibly describe the same event from different perspectives and with varying detail. This is how God chose to have His Son's biographies penned by Matthew, Mark, Luke, and John. Each describes the life and ministry of Jesus Christ from different angles. John is distinct because it is built around key themes in Jesus' life; Matthew, Mark, and Luke are built around key events in His life (more or less chronologically). These three are called the *synoptic Gospels.* *Synoptic* is from a Greek word meaning "to view together or to summarize," and *Gospel* is from an Old English word for "glad tidings or the good news of Jesus Christ."

Interestingly, none of the synoptic Gospels bears an internal reference to the author's name or the name of the original recipients. Long-standing church tradition and conservative scholarship (based on a variety of evidences) attribute the three books to the men whose names they've borne since the second century.

- Matthew: likely written first (between A.D. 50–75), is attributed to one of the original apostles, "Matthew the tax collector" (Matt. 10:3), also known as "Levi the *son of* Alphaeus" (Mark 2:14).
- Mark: likely written between A.D. 65–70, is attributed to "John whose surname was Mark" (Acts 12:12), a close "son" to Peter (1 Pet. 5:13).
- Luke: likely written between A.D. 59–75 as the first of two volumes, Luke-Acts (Acts 1:1), is attributed to "Luke the beloved physician" (Col. 4:14), a close fellow

laborer with Paul and the only known Gentile author of a New Testament book.

The Gospels themselves indicate to students of the New Testament world who they were primarily written for and why. "Matthew is full of clues that it was [largely] written to convince Jewish readers that Jesus is the Messiah. Mark is evidently written for Gentiles, and for Romans in particular . . . to portray Jesus as God's Son. . . . Luke has the most universal outlook of all the Gospels . . . [portraying] Jesus as a man with compassion for all peoples."[1]

JESUS CHRIST'S ROOTS

Two of the Gospels, Matthew and Luke, begin with events leading to the Christmas story. Both Gospels open similarly, summarizing Jesus' family roots.

Read Matthew 1:1–17 and Luke 3:23–38 and note the following.

How far back do Matthew and Luke go in tracing Jesus' genealogy? (As we continue our study, look for the way these genealogies reinforce each writer's purpose.)

How does Luke handle the fact that Joseph was Jesus' legal father but not His biological father? (3:23; see Matt. 1:18)

"Specifically stating that Jesus was the supposed son of Joseph, Luke ascends the family line all the way to Adam, thus identifying Jesus universally with the human race."[2]

Matthew mentions David five times, Luke only once. According to Matthew 9:27, 12:23, 21:9, and 22:42, who were the people expecting the Christ to be?

BEHIND THE SCENES

God promised David everlasting rulership through his seed (Ps. 89:29). Over 200 years later, Isaiah prophesied this Davidic descendant, "Of the increase of *His* government and peace *there will be* no end, upon the throne of David and over His kingdom, to order it and establish it with judgment and justice from that time forward, even forever" (Is. 9:7).

In Jesus' day at least some branches of popular Judaism understood "son of David" to be messianic. God's promises, though long delayed, had not been forgotten; Jesus and his ministry were perceived as God's fulfillment of covenantal promises now centuries old. The tree of David, hacked off so that only a stump remained, was sprouting a new branch (Is. 11:1).[3]

What other name does Matthew give to Jesus to reinforce this messianic anointing? (vv. 1, 16)

WORD WEALTH

Jesus, *Iesous,* is the Greek rendering of the Hebrew *Yeshua,* "He Shall Save," which is the shorter form of *Yehoshua* (Joshua), "Yahweh Is Salvation." It was a common male Jewish name. Ten men in the Old Testament are named *Yeshua,* and three men besides the Lord in the New Testament are so named.

Christ, *Christos,* or the Anointed One, comes from the verb *chrio,* "to anoint," referring to the consecration rites of a priest or king. *Christos* translates the Hebrew *Mashiyach,* "Messiah." Unfortunately, the transliteration of *Christos* into English, resulting in the word "Christ," deprives the word of much of its meaning. It would be better to translate *Christos* in every instance as "the Anointed One" or "the Messiah," denoting a title. "Jesus Christ" actually means Jesus the Messiah, or Jesus the Anointed One, emphasizing the fact that the man Jesus was God's Anointed One, the promised Messiah.[4]

Luke ends his genealogy by calling Adam "the_____
_____" (3:38). Since this is Jesus' genealogy, what do
you infer from this way of concluding? What does Gabriel
announce to Mary that corresponds with this description of
Adam? (1:32)

Leon Morris comments that "Luke adds *the son of God*
[3:38], for we must see Jesus ultimately in his relationship to
the Father. In this the genealogy harmonizes with the preceding and the following narratives, both of which are concerned
with Jesus as the Son of God."[5]

At a Glance

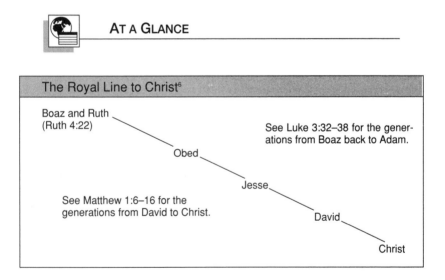

The Royal Line to Christ[6]

Boaz and Ruth
(Ruth 4:22)

See Luke 3:32–38 for the generations from Boaz back to Adam.

Obed

Jesse

See Matthew 1:6–16 for the
generations from David to Christ.

David

Christ

The Annunciation

The concept is almost beyond human comprehension. In
fulfillment of centuries of prophetic promises going back to
the first messianic prophecy (Gen. 3:15), "the Word became
flesh and dwelt among us" (John 1:14). "When the fullness of
the time had come, God sent forth His Son, born of a
woman" (Gal. 4:4); Christ "made Himself of no reputation,

taking the form of a bondservant, and coming in the likeness of men" (Phil. 2:7). "The Bible teaches that our Savior was both fully divine and completely human during His earthly life. But nowhere does Scripture explain exactly how Jesus' two natures co-existed. [It] does not say that Jesus stopped being God or that He gave up any divine attributes. While not ceasing to be God's Son, Christ also became God's Servant.[7]

It all begins in Nazareth of Galilee with a young virgin named Mary, engaged to Joseph. Read Luke 1:26–38 and answer the following.

Who makes the announcement to Mary? (v. 26)

How does he greet Mary? (v. 28) What's her response? (v. 29)

Why is she chosen? (v. 30)

What is Gabriel's specific announcement to her? (v. 31)

What is Mary's initial response? (v. 34) Gabriel's answer? (v. 35)

What is Mary's final response? (v. 38)

Immediately following this encounter, "Mary arose . . . and went into the hill country with haste . . . and greeted Elizabeth," her cousin (Luke 1:39–56). Elizabeth is now six months pregnant with John the Baptist, whose life will be highlighted in our next chapter. "Mary remained with her about three months" (v. 56).

Of major importance to the visit is the *Magnificat* (from its opening word in St. Jerome's Latin Bible), otherwise known as "The Song of Mary" (Luke 1:46–55). It is a sponta-neous hymn of praise in response to Elizabeth's shouted benediction, "Blessed are you among women, and blessed is the fruit of your womb!" (1:42). It is filled with Old Testament language and quotes, which the young Mary would have known as a Jewish believer. "There are several resemblances to the song of Hannah (1 Sam. 2:1–10). But there is a difference in tone. Hannah's song is a shout of triumph in the face of her enemies, Mary's a humble contemplation of the mercies of God."[8]

Read Luke 1:46–55 and answer the following.

How does Mary declare her gratitude at being used by God? (vv. 46–47)

What is the basis for her magnifying and rejoicing? (vv. 48–49)

What three attributes of God does Mary magnify? (vv. 49–50)

The second half of the Song (vv. 51–55) is built around a frequent Old Testament image, "He has shown strength with His arm" (see Ex. 6:1–6 and Is. 51:5). List the six specifics in which Mary sees God intervening.

BEHIND THE SCENES

In the original *koine* Greek of the New Testament, the main verbs in Luke 1:51–55 ("has shown," "has scattered," "has put down," "has filled," "has sent away," "has helped") are in the "aorist" (*air*-ist) tense. It usually denotes completed past action; however, here the tense is predictive. "[Mary] is [likely] looking forward in a spirit of prophecy and counting what God will do as so certain that it can be spoken of as accomplished (this is frequent in the Old Testament prophets)."[9]

FAITH ALIVE

Though probably but a teenager, Mary exemplifies devotion and piety amidst very trying God-ordained circumstances. How about you? If given an assignment of her magnitude, would you be able to say freely as she did, "Let it be to me according to Your word" (Luke 1:38)? Do you think your soul would magnify the Lord and your spirit rejoice, or would you likely be tempted to be depressed, overwhelmed, or resistant? The angel says to her, "Rejoice, highly favored *one*" (Luke 1:28), and apparently she does. Do you believe you're one of God's favored, worthy of a noble assignment? Assess these matters in prayer and let the Spirit speak to your heart. Any areas which might need growth, commit to pray, and study God's word until enlightenment comes to your heart.

LET'S NOT FORGET JOSEPH!

What about Joseph in all this? Both Matthew (1:18) and Luke (1:27) tell us that he and Mary were betrothed (legally engaged). Scholar John Nolland notes that "in Jewish tradition a girl was normally betrothed in the thirteenth year and for legal but not domestic purposes was from that point on considered to be married. Around a year later the girl was taken to the bridegroom's home for normal married life to begin. Sexual relations prior to this 'taking home' would be considered a violation of marriage customs."[10]

Read Matthew 1:18–25 and note Joseph's response to the news about Mary's pregnancy.

What does Joseph initially resolve to do? (v. 19)

How does God persuade him otherwise? (vv. 20–23)

The angel (vv. 22–23) says Mary's situation is the fulfillment of the messianic prophecy in Isaiah 7:14. What is that prophecy?

KINGDOM EXTRA

The dual reference of the Immanuel prophecy of Isaiah 7 often goes unnoticed. It was a prophetic sign "to Ahaz as an assurance of Judah's hope in the midst of adversity. It therefore had an immediate, historical fulfillment. Its usage in the New Testament shows that it also had a messianic fulfillment. The Hebrew word for **virgin** (*'almah*) means either a 'virgin' or a 'young woman' of marriageable age. Isaiah's readers could have understood it to be either. Messianically, it irrefutably refers to the Virgin Mary (Matt. 1:23; Luke 1:27), where the Greek *parthenos* (virgin) removes any question."[11]

How does Joseph respond to the dream (v. 24) and how long does Mary remain a virgin? (v. 25)

THE BIRTH AND ADORATION OF JESUS CHRIST

Luke alone records the details of Jesus' birth. Read Luke 2:1–20 and note the following.

How does God see to it that Mary is in Bethlehem for the birth, to fulfill Micah 5:2?

Caesar Augustus was emperor from 30 B.C. until A.D. 14. Quirinius was governor of Syria during 10–7 B.C. and later served a second term during A.D. 6–9. Because "Jesus was born in Bethlehem of Judea in the days of Herod the king" (Matt. 2:1), and because Herod died in the early spring of 4 B.C., Jesus was born before 4 B.C. When the wise men came to visit Jesus He was a young Child (Matt. 2:1, 8), making Jesus' birth likely early in the year 5 B.C.

Everett Harrison observes that "Scripture says nothing about the time of year. The first known observance of December 25th is associated with the church at Rome about the middle of the fourth century, but the practice may go back to the second century. January 6 was observed in the Eastern churches."[12]

Sheep were kept in the open fields (Luke 2:8) between March and December.

Where is Jesus born and why? (v. 7)

Swaddling cloths were strips of cloth used to wrap infants; a manger was an animal feeding trough.

To whom is Jesus' birth first announced and who announces it? (vv. 8–9)

What do the angels say to help the shepherds recognize the Savior? (vv. 11–12)

What are the shepherds' responses upon seeing Him? (vv. 17, 20)

BEHIND THE SCENES

Among the occupations, shepherding had a lowly place. Shepherds were considered untrustworthy and their work made them ceremonially unclean. Thus the most obvious implication is that the gospel first came to the social outcasts of Jesus' day. In both testaments shepherds [also] symbolize those who care for God's people, including the Lord himself (Ps. 23:1; Is. 40:11; I Pet. 2:25). The shepherds of Luke 2 may, therefore, symbolize all the ordinary people who have joyfully received the gospel and have become in various ways pastors to others.[13]

Matthew records another early adoration of the Savior, the wise men from the East (2:1–12). It is similar to the royal visit of the Queen of Sheba to Solomon (I Kin. 10:1–12), which was a form of homage and gift bearing to a son of David, a king of the Jews.

Whom are they seeking and why? How do they know how to get as far as Jerusalem? (v. 2)

 BEHIND THE SCENES

The wise men are not easy to identify. The Greek word for wise men in this account (*magoi*) is rendered as "astrologers" where it occurs in the SEPTUAGINT, the Greek translation of the Old Testament (Dan. 1:20; 2:2) and as "sorcerer" in its other occurrences in the New Testament (Acts 13:6, 8).

The Greek historian Herodotus, writing in the fifth century B.C., identified the Magi as a caste of Medes who had a priestly function in the Persian Empire. In the Book of Daniel the "astrologers" (*magoi*) are grouped with magicians, sorcerers, and Chaldeans as advisers to the court of Babylon with responsibility for interpreting dreams.

The role of the star in Matthew 2 suggests a connection with astrology. These astrologers, pursuing their observations of the stars in the heavens, encountered a sign of God (Matt. 24:29–30). God broke through their misguided system to make the great event known.

The joy, rejoicing, worship, and gifts which mark the response of these wise men to the birth of Jesus is quite a contrast to the troubled state and murderous intent of Herod and his Jewish advisers in Jerusalem (Matt. 2:1–12).[14]

In contrast to the wise men's desire to worship Jesus, what is Herod's initial response? (v. 3) What does he pretend is in his heart? (v. 8)

God knows Herod is insincere and warns the wise men
_____ . (v. 12)

According to Matthew 2:1–12, does the star stay illuminated during their entire journey?

The exact nature of the star is a mystery. Matthew obviously conveys a supernatural occurrence and probably an allusion to Balaam's prophecy that "a Star shall come out of Jacob" (Num. 24:17). Perhaps the wise men were familiar with this prophecy, which stirred them to go to Jerusalem. Astronomers tell us that between 7–4 B.C. a conjunction of the planets Jupiter and Saturn gave the appearance of a bright star near the earth, but Matthew does not tell us how this star occurred. Many Bible scholars think that this star was an angelic visitation, and several biblical passages seem to link stars to angels (see Job 38:7; Is. 14:13; Rev. 12:4).

Where do the wise men find Jesus?

OBEDIENCE TO JEWISH LAW

It is Luke (2:21–40) who records two events that show Joseph and Mary to be pious Jews. These two events happen prior to the visit of the wise men by possibly as much as twelve to fifteen months.

In accordance with Gen. 17:12, what happens to Jesus when He is eight days old?

In accordance with Leviticus 12:1–5, what do Joseph and Mary do thirty-three days later? (v. 24)

In accordance with Numbers 18:15, what do they do at the same time? (vv. 22–23)

These two ceremonies are distinct for two different reasons, but there is no Levitical prohibition against combining them in a single visit to the temple.

Who greets them in the temple, and what does he do? (vv. 25–28)

What is the focus of Simeon's praise? (vv. 29–32)

On a more somber note, what does Simeon prophesy to Mary? (vv. 34, 35)

Who else does God have waiting to see Jesus, and what does she do? (v. 38)

Although the original Greek meaning is obscure, it is probably best to take "this woman was a widow of about eighty-four years" (v. 37) to mean that Anna is eighty-four at the time, and not that she has been a widow for eighty-four years.

1. "Luke, Gospel of," "Mark, Gospel of," "Matthew, Gospel of," *Nelson's Illustrated Bible Dictionary* (Nashville: Thomas Nelson, 1986), 660, 678, 688.
2. *Spirit-Filled Life Bible* (Nashville: Thomas Nelson, 1991), note on Luke 3:23–38.
3. Frank E. Gaebelein, ed., *The Expositor's Bible Commentary*, Vol. 8 (Grand Rapids: Zondervan, 1984), 62. Used by permission.
4. *Spirit-Filled Life Bible*, 1808, "Word Wealth: Phil. 4:23 Jesus"; 1858, "Word Wealth: 2 Tim. 4:22 Christ."
5. Leon Morris, *Tyndale New Testament Commentaries: Luke* (Grand Rapids: Eerdmans, 1990), 111. Used by permission.
6. *The Wesley Study Bible* (Nashville: Thomas Nelson, 1990), 383.
7. "Kenosis," *Nelson's Illustrated Bible Dictionary*, 613.
8. Morris, *Luke*, 83.
9. Ibid., 85.
10. John Nolland, *Word Biblical Commentary: Luke* (Dallas: Word, 1989), 49. Used by permission.
11. *Spirit-Filled Life Bible*, note on Isa. 7:14.
12. Everett Harrison, *A Short Life of Christ* (Grand Rapids: Eerdmans, 1977), 39. Used by permission.
13. Gaebelein, 845.
14. "Wise Men," *Nelson's Illustrated Bible Dictionary*, 1104.

Lesson 2/The Heavens Were Opened to Him

Luke tells us, "Jesus Himself began His ministry at about thirty years of age" (Luke 3:23). The year is about A.D. 27. The Bible is relatively silent about the years between His birth and public ministry. There are only two major events recorded. Matthew tells us that shortly after the visit of the Magi, Herod is infuriated and tries to have the young Child destroyed (Matt. 2:13–18). God warns Joseph in a dream to take the family to Egypt for safety. This flight to Egypt ties Jesus' life to that of Moses and becomes a messianic fulfillment of Hosea 11:1. Following an unspecified time in Egypt, the family returns to Israel (after Herod's death), and they make their way to Nazareth in the district of Galilee (Matt. 2:19–23).

The second event occurs when Jesus is twelve years old (Luke 2:41–52). The family has gone to Jerusalem for its annual celebration of Passover. Afterwards, on the journey home, they discover that Jesus is not traveling with them. Joseph and Mary supposed Jesus was somewhere in the company (v. 44). It takes them three days to find Him. He's still in the temple in discussions with the rabbis. He stayed behind to be about His Father's business (v. 50). (This is the last time we hear directly of Joseph.)

Luke summarizes Jesus' next eighteen years by saying He was subject to His parents "and . . . increased in wisdom and stature, and in favor with God and men" (vv. 51–52). We can assume that during this time Jesus learns His trade, assisting Joseph as village carpenter (Matt. 13:55; Mark 6:3). "Carpenter" (*tekton*) is used for manual labor with metal, stone, or wood.

Jesus' entrance into messianic ministry at age thirty is through a public water baptism, through which God affirms who Jesus is and His mission. (This is where Mark begins his account.) Jesus' baptism is followed immediately by satanic temptations in the Judean wilderness. In this chapter, we'll explore Christ's baptism and temptations; but first we must look at a key player in Jesus' public inauguration, John the son of Zacharias (Luke 3:2), commonly called John the Baptist (Matt. 3:1).

AT A GLANCE

The Journeys of Jesus' Birth. Fulfillment of prophecy was involved both when Joseph and Mary went to Bethlehem (Mic. 5:2), obeying the imperial decree (Luke 2:1–5), and when they went to Egypt (Hos. 11:1), following the angel's command (Matt. 2:13).[1]

MIRACULOUSLY BORN, PROPHETICALLY CALLED

John is six months older than Jesus and their mothers are relatives (Luke 1:36). Though not immaculate, John's birth is miraculous. It's announced by an angel and comes late in his parents' lives, his mother having been barren for years. Read Luke, chapter 1.

What are his parents' names and lineage? (v. 5)

So as not to confuse Elizabeth's barrenness with a chastisement from God, what are we told about Zechariah and Elizabeth? (v. 6)

Where is Zechariah when Elizabeth is told she will conceive? To what does the angel attribute the miracle? (vv. 8–13)

What is going to be unique about John? (v. 15)

 BEHIND THE SCENES

Wine and strong drink are often linked in the Old Testament (see Lev. 10:9; Num. 6:3). "Strong drink" (Greek, *sikera*) refers to an alcoholic drink not made with grapes, especially beer. Some have seen the angel announcing that John is to be a Nazirite (Num. 6:1–8), but this is never stated; furthermore, there is no mention of the Nazirite requirement for not cutting one's hair. It's likely that this is the way John is being called to a unique life-style, partly that of a priest and partly that of a Nazirite.

"He will also be filled with the Holy Spirit" (Luke 1:15) is best understood as a "pre-natal" rather than a "from birth" filling (see vv. 41, 44). It's also best understood in the New Testament sense of the Holy Spirit permanently residing with John for empowerment (see Eph. 5:18), rather than simply coming upon him for a task as with the Old Testament prophets (see I Sam. 10:10; 2 Sam. 23:2).

What is John's mission? (vv. 16–17)

According to Luke 1:18, how does Zechariah respond to this announcement? How do we know this is not a simple inquiry (v. 20), similar to that of Mary's? (v. 34)

In the spirit of Rachel (Gen. 30:23), how does Elizabeth respond to the pregnancy? (v. 25)

At John's circumcision and naming (vv. 59–66), Zechariah's "mouth was opened . . . and he spoke, praising God" (v. 64). He then prophesied (vv. 67–79), and his prophecy is called *The Benedictus* (from its first word in the Latin Bible). It links the roles of Jesus Christ and John the Baptist.

List the reasons why Zechariah says, "Blessed is the Lord God of Israel" (vv. 68–75).

Zechariah sees Jesus' coming as a fulfillment of a promise going back to whom? (v. 73; see Gen. 22:16–17)

What is John the Baptist's prophesied role in God's messianic plan? (vv. 76–77)

A BAPTISM OF REPENTANCE

Sometime between A.D. 25–27, John begins his public ministry (Luke 3:1–2). All three of the synoptic writers mention his ministry, and that it's a fulfillment of the words of Isaiah the prophet (Luke 3:4; see Is. 40:3–5).

Where does John conduct his ministry? (Luke 3:3)

Why is his mission as a herald of the Messiah? (Luke 3:3–5)

WORD WEALTH

Repent, *metanoeo;* from *meta,* "after", and *noeo,* "to think." Repentance is a decision that results in a change of mind, which in turn leads to a change of purpose and action.[2] "Connoted a whole-hearted 'return to Yahweh' and taking Yahweh seriously as 'Israel's God.' Such an abandoning of one's wrong ways and a return to God's ways in obedient surrender belonged to the prophetic hope for the age of salvation (see Mal. 4:5–6; Ezek. 11:19; 36:25–26; Dan. 9:13)."[3]

What are John's dress and diet? (Mark 1:6)

John's dress and diet are those of desert nomads. They also "marked him out as being in the rugged tradition of Elijah and the other desert prophets (see 2 Kin. 1:8)," according to commentator R. Alan Cole.[4]

John's ministry arouses tremendous response and curiosity (Matt. 3:7–10; Luke 3:7–14). In the midst of this, what is John's great concern? (Luke 3:8)

How does John describe his point about the seriousness of one's need to "bear fruits worthy of repentance"? (Luke 3:9)

BIBLE EXTRA

To be baptized is to be immersed into something or someone. John states that Jesus "will baptize . . . with the Holy Spirit" (Matt. 3:12). Thus the Holy Spirit will be "put into" believers. In one sense, therefore, the baptism with the Holy Spirit is indicative of actual forgiveness of sins. By proclaiming a repentance-baptism and pointing to a Spirit-baptism, John fulfills Isaiah 40:3, the task of the "voice of one crying in the wilderness to prepare the way of the Lord."[5] (See Ezek. 36:25–27; 39:29 and Joel 2:28.)

For individual believers in Jesus Christ, what does the truth that Jesus will baptize us with the Holy Spirit and fire mean?

In a few sentences recount when and how Jesus Christ baptized you with the Holy Spirit.

If you cannot recount a time when you were baptized in the Holy Spirit, look up Acts 1:4–8 and 2:38–39 to discover how Jesus Christ's promise is to you also.

BEHIND THE SCENES

Scholars are divided in understanding John's statement that Jesus "will baptize . . . with the Holy Spirit and fire" (Matt. 3:11). The Greek grammar in this sentence closely connects the Holy Spirit and the fire; hence, as Morris points out, it's probably "best to see John as thinking of positive and negative aspects of Messiah's message. Those who accept him will be purified as by fire (see Mal. 3:1–3) and strengthened by the Holy Spirit."[6]

JESUS' WATER BAPTISM

Now about 30 years old, Jesus steps from His "ordinary" life as a young Jewish carpenter to His destiny as Messiah. He chooses John's baptism as the commissioning point for His messianic ministry (Matt. 3:13). He is baptized publicly in the Jordan River, One among many of John's candidates (Luke 3:21). Let's look at Matthew's account (3:13–17), the most detailed in the Synoptics.

What is John's reaction when Jesus comes for baptism? (v. 14)

What is Jesus' reason for being baptized by John? (v. 15)

"To fulfill all righteousness" (v. 15) likely refers to Jesus sub-mitting to God's will at this point in His life. In particular, He accepts His destiny as Israel's Suffering Servant by identifying through John's baptism with those whom He will later redeem.

What happens when Jesus came up from the water? (v. 16)

If Jesus Christ, the Son of God, chose to be baptized, what does this say about the need for water baptism by indi-vidual believers?

The descending of the Spirit upon Him is in keeping with prophetic promise (Is. 11:2; 42:1; 61:1). The Spirit's role in Jesus' messianic mission becomes particularly important in Luke's account of Jesus' ministry.

What two realities does "a voice . . . from heaven" affirm? (v. 17)

The voice is probably heard only by Jesus (see Mark's and Luke's "You are . . ."). This is His commissioning by the Father, not a public announcement of His sonship or messiah-ship. Read Psalm 2:7 and Isaiah 42:1 to see how Matthew 3:17 compares.

R. T. France correctly points out that "There is no sug-gestion Jesus *became* Son of God at his baptism. It was a piv-otal experience, not in that it made Jesus anything which he was not already, but in that it launched him on the mission for which he had long prepared, and defined that mission in terms of Old Testament expectation."[7]

"'The heavens were opened to Him,'" adds Jack Hayford, "doesn't mean the sky opened up, but that the invisible realm of spiritual reality became more vivid, to give spiritual insight for the purpose of ministering to others."[8]

TEMPTATION IN THE WILDERNESS

The plan of God immediately calls for Jesus to face Satan in the wilderness. The intensity and necessity of the encounter are particularly portrayed by Mark, who says the Spirit *drove* Him into the wilderness (1:12). It is generally agreed that the primary purposes of Jesus' temptations are to portray from the outset His victory over the kingdom of darkness and His victory as the last Adam in contrast to the failing first Adam. Jesus the Messiah must bind the strong man (Mark 3:26–27), while identifying with humankind in its battle with temptation (Heb. 2:17–18).

AT A GLANCE

TEMPTATION: THE TWO ADAMS CONTRASTED[9]		
Both Adam and Christ faced three aspects of temptation. Adam yielded, bringing upon humankind sin and death. Christ resisted, resulting in justification and life.		
1 John 2:16	Genesis 3:6 First Adam	Luke 4:1–13 Second Adam—Christ
"the lust of the flesh"	"the tree was good for food"	"command this stone to become bread"
"the lust of the eyes"	"it was pleasant to the eyes"	"the devil . . . showed Him all the kingdoms"
"the pride of life"	"a tree desirable to make one wise"	"throw yourself down from here"

Let's study Luke's account of the temptation (4:1–13).

What is Jesus' relationship to the Holy Spirit at this important time in His ministry? (v. 1)

What is His purpose for being "led . . . into the wilderness"? (v. 1)

This region may have been the one in which John the Baptist conducted his ministry. It also symbolically represents a place away from all human provision and support, where Israel failed many testings, and where the messianic mission is prophesied to originate (Is. 40:3).

How long is Jesus in the wilderness? (v. 2)

The forty days are likely a microcosm of Israel's forty years in the wilderness. They also recall the experience of Moses (Ex. 24:18) and Elijah (1 Kin. 19:8, 15).

Mark adds an interesting detail in 1:13. What is it?

The "wild beasts" (Mark 1:3) add to the fierceness of the experience; they are occasionally associated with evil (see Ps. 91; Ezek. 34). Jesus' peaceful co-existence with them also foreshadows a future messianic blessing (Is. 11:6–9; 65:17–25).

Luke notes that the devil tempts Jesus during the entire forty days (Luke 4:2), and that he will continue to do so throughout His ministry (v. 13). Three of the temptations are mentioned in detail.

What is the first temptation and what is Jesus' physical condition? (vv. 2–3) What does Satan seem to be tempting?

"If" in the original Greek (*ei*) does not connote doubt; it could be translated *since*. *The Expositor's Bible Commentary* notes that "Satan was not inviting Jesus to doubt His sonship but to reflect on its meaning. Sonship of the living God, he suggested, surely means Jesus has the power and right to satisfy his own needs."[10]

How does Jesus end the temptation? (v. 4)

What is the second temptation and what is its purpose? (vv. 5–7)

Commentator John Nolland observes that wherever evil is found, there Satan's influence is present. "Satan's role in this situation does not relate specifically to Satan worship. The worship of Satan to which Jesus is enticed is the temptation to pursue His task in the ways of the world . . . to gain glory for himself in this world by compromise with the forces that control it . . . and to become indebted to Satan in the manner that every successful man of the world is."[11]

We do not know why Matthew and Luke differ in the order of the second and third temptations. Most scholars feel Matthew's order is the original and that Luke changed them because he wants the climax in Jerusalem, where Jesus' ministry will end (see 9:51; 13:32–33).

How does Jesus end the temptation? (v. 8)

What principal resource does Jesus use to win victory over temptation? How can we use it in our own lives? (vv. 4, 8)

If Jesus Christ, the Son of God, was tempted by Satan, what can we as modern-day disciples of Jesus Christ expect?

How does the knowledge that we can expect temptation, as we seek to follow God, help to prepare us? (1 Cor. 10:13)

     WORD WEALTH

Tempt, *peirazo,* from the Greek verb "to explore, test, try, assay, examine, prove, attempt, tempt. [It] describes the testing of the believer's loyalty, strength, opinions, disposition, condition, faith, patience, or character. *Peirazo* determines which way one is going and what one is made of."[12]

FAITH ALIVE

Jesus' primary defense against Satan's temptation was God's rightly divided word from Deuteronomy 6—8, which was obviously hidden in His heart. How would you evaluate your knowledge of God's word?

How well do you understand and have committed to memory key biblical truths, such as how to deal with temptation and how to make yourself fully available to God to live daily life so that He is pleased?

In what areas or circumstances of your life do you feel the tug of temptation most strongly?

What help does Psalm 119:11 offer you in your struggle with temptation and against sin?

1. *Spirit-Filled Life Bible* (Nashville: Thomas Nelson, 1991), 1406.
2. *Spirit-Filled Life Bible*, 1407, "Word Wealth: Matt. 3:2 repent."
3. Robert Guelich, *Word Biblical Commentary: Mark* (Dallas: Word, 1989), 19. Used by permission.
4. R. Alan Cole, *Tyndale New Testament Commentaries: Mark* (Grand Rapids: Eerdmans, 1989), 107. Used by permission.
5. Guelich, *Mark*, 27.
6. Leon Morris, *Tyndale New Testament Commentaries: Luke* (Grand Rapids: Eerdmans, 1990), 107.
7. R. T. France, *Tyndale New Testament Commentaries: Matthew* (Grand Rapids: Eerdmans, 1986), 96. Used by permission.
8. Jack Hayford, *Water Baptism: Sealed by Christ, the Lord* (Van Nuys, Calif.: Living Way Ministries, 1984), 11.
9. *Spirit-Filled Life Bible*, 1515.
10. Frank E. Gaebelein, ed., *The Expositor's Bible Commentary*, Vol. 8 (Grand Rapids: Zondervan, 1984), 112.
11. John Nolland, *Word Biblical Commentary: Luke*, (Dallas: Word, 1989), 180.
12. *Spirit-Filled Life Bible*, 1963, "Word Wealth: Rev. 2:10 tested."

Lesson 3/ The Kingdom of God Proclaimed

Have you ever wondered if the Bible holds a theological key to understanding it? Of course, Jesus Christ is *the* key. But is there a concept that could make much of the Bible "fall into place"? Indeed there is: the concept of the kingdom of God.

There is no full agreement, even among evangelicals, as to nuances of the meaning of the kingdom of God. But enough is clear that we may discuss it with confidence, even when we cannot clarify all we would like to.

The next few chapters of this study will focus on various aspects of the kingdom of God as seen and taught in the life and ministry of Jesus.

 WORD WEALTH

Kingdom, Hebrew, *malkut;* Greek, *basileia.* Both words are usually translated "kingdom" in our English Bibles and mean kingdom, kingship, royal power, royal rule, royal dominion, or royal reign. The kingdom of God[1] thus denotes the sovereign lordship, or reign, of God over His people and over the universe. "One thing is certain," comments the outstanding scholar Joachim Jeremias, kingdom "did not have for the Oriental the significance that the word 'kingdom' does for the Westerner. Only in quite isolated instances . . . does it denote a realm in the spatial sense, a territory; almost always it stands for the government, the authority, the power of a king. The kingdom of God [then] is neither a spatial nor a static concept; it is a *dynamic concept.* It denotes the reign of God in action, in the first place as opposed to earthly monarchy, but then in contrast to all rule in heaven and on earth."[2]

GOD'S KINGDOM IN THE OLD TESTAMENT

God's sovereignty as Supreme King of the universe is assumed in Gen. 1:1 when Moses declares, "In the beginning God created the heavens and the earth." Only a preexistent Supreme One could so create.

What do each of the following scriptures declare about God's supreme royal reign?

1 Chr. 29:10–13

Ps. 145:10–13

Dan. 4:34–35

The Lord's royal reign is clearly seen in human history. Following creation, God does not abandon earth; He remains its Sovereign Ruler. As such He exercises general, overall sovereign rulership *and* He reigns uniquely in and through His people (primarily Israel in the Old Testament).

What is God's original plan for humankind and His royal rule over creation? (Gen. 1:26–28)

What happened at the Fall to the rule God delegated to humankind? (Gen. 3:8–24; see also Eph. 2:1–2; 1 John 5:19)

Genesis 12:1–3 records God's first move to establish a covenant people who will become unique vessels for His reign on earth. It is about 1950 B.C. Who is to be the head of this new people, and how will God's reign be manifest to him and through him?

How do we see God's reign operating through Moses? (Ex. 7—11)

Nearly 1,000 years after delegating His reign through Abraham, what special promise does God make to Abraham's descendant, David (1 Chr. 17:10–15)?

GOD'S KINGDOM IN THE NEW TESTAMENT

Between the Old and New Testaments, Israel's expectation of God's reign coming to her through the Messiah heightens. Israel looks eagerly for God to break into human history to judge evil, bring about repentance, and establish an earthly, Davidic monarchy to overthrow her political enemies. Against this backdrop John the Baptist appears, proclaiming, "Repent, for the kingdom of heaven is at hand!" (Matt. 3:2).

Within months of beginning His public ministry, Jesus begins His Galilean tour "preaching the gospel of the kingdom of God, and saying, 'The time is fulfilled, and the kingdom of God is at hand. Repent, and believe in the gospel'" (Mark 1:14–15). Jesus reveals here that to preach the good news of the gospel is to preach the message of the kingdom of God: they are the same message. This is why Matthew says that "Jesus went about all Galilee, teaching in their synagogues, preaching the gospel of the kingdom" (Matt. 4:23). It is why Paul summarizes his ministry in Ephesus as, "among [you] I have gone preaching the kingdom of God" (Acts 20:25).

BIBLE EXTRA

"The name and message of Jesus Christ, of Jesus Christ Himself, are equated with the kingdom of God. For Jesus, the invading kingdom of God has come into time and the world in His person, as expressed by John in the statement 'the Word became flesh' (John 1:14). We can thus see why the apostolic and post-apostolic church of the New Testament did not speak much of the 'kingdom of God' explicitly, but always emphasized it implicitly by its reference to the 'Lord Jesus Christ.' It is not true that it now substituted the church for the kingdom as preached by Jesus of Nazareth. On the contrary, faith in the kingdom of God persists in the post-Easter experience of Christ."[3]

One of the first cities to hear about the kingdom of God is Nazareth. Read Luke 4:16–21 and note the following.

Which prophet does Jesus read? (v. 17)

By whom will the Messiah teach and demonstrate the message of the kingdom? (v. 18; see 3:21–22)

Quoting Isaiah, what does Luke mention as part of the Messiah's kingdom message and ministry? (vv. 18–19)

It is generally agreed, from examining Jesus' ministry, that Isaiah's prophecy refers to those in need both spiritually and physically. Jesus releases a boy from demonic captivity (Luke 9:37–43); He opens Bartimaeus's physically blind eyes (Mark 10:46–52); He opens Saul's spiritually blind eyes (Acts 9:1–19); He relieves a downtrodden mother's oppression (Luke 7:11–17).

When does Jesus see this ministry as beginning? (v. 21)

How does Acts 10:38 fulfill the prophecy of Isaiah 61:1–3?

As believers in Jesus Christ, who are also anointed with the Holy Spirit, what does Acts 10:38 and Isaiah 61:1–3 say about the way we should minister to others?

BEHIND THE SCENES

"The acceptable year of the Lord" (Luke 4:19) means the year that God has graciously appointed to demonstrate His salvation. I. Howard Marshall explains: "Concretely, the allusion is to the 'year of jubilee,' the year of liberation among men appointed by Yahweh (Lev. 25) and now made symbolic of his own saving acts. It was held every fifty years, and during it the fields lay fallow, persons returned to their own homes, debts were relinquished and slaves set free."[4]

PROBING THE DEPTHS

Jesus knew that many Jews expected that the coming of God's kingdom would establish Israel as the superpower of the earth and would also annihilate evil. But He also knew that they misunderstood His mission and how God's reign would be inaugurated. They did not understand that God would send His Son to be the Messiah, or that the Messiah would die for the sins of the world and then be resurrected. Furthermore, the Jews did not comprehend that the Messiah would then return to the right hand of God and delay the consummation of God's reign until He (the Messiah) returned to earth a second time, fulfilling the prophetic scriptures.

WORD WEALTH

Because the Jews misunderstood how God's kingdom would be established, Jesus called it a **mystery**, which in the Greek is *musterion,* from *mueo,* which means "to initiate into the mysteries." In the New Testament the word denotes something people could never know by their own understanding and that demands a revelation from God.[5] Thus Jesus tells His disciples, "To you it has been given to know the mystery of the kingdom of God" (Mark 4:11).

KEY KINGDOM PARABLES

As stated in Mark 4, Jesus uses parables to teach about the kingdom of God. In particular, there are eight major kingdom parables, seven in Matthew 13 and one in Mark 4. These illustrate what God's royal reign in Jesus Christ is like.

WORD WEALTH

Parable, *parabole.* A placing beside, a comparison. Parables are short fictitious narratives based on familiar experiences and have an application to the spiritual life. They arouse thought and require humility to grasp. "About one-third of Jesus' teaching was in parables. . . . In interpreting parables, one must guard against fanciful allegorization of details, staying primarily with the major point of the story. [Yet] Jesus' own interpretation [of the Parable of the Soils] demonstrates that the details of a parable can indeed hold symbolic significance and application."[6]

THE FOUR SOILS

Read Matthew 13:1–9, 18–23 and answer the following.

Luke's parallel passage states, "The seed is the word of God" (8:11). Matthew is more specific, calling it _____ _____ (v. 19).

Jesus states four responses to God's reign. What are they?

v. 19

v. 20

v. 22

v. 23

Jesus states that three of these responses ultimately bear no fruit. List the reasons why.

v. 19

v. 21

v. 22

What results in the life of those who hear the Word and understand it? (v. 23)

To what does Luke attribute this response? (Luke 8:15)

What would you conclude is Jesus' main point?

Many Jewish people were awaiting a sudden, violent inbreaking of divine power that would nearly instantly destroy all evil and evil powers. Who would have expected the kingdom's coming through a Servant who would rather quietly invade human history and cripple the forces of evil, not by human might or power but by the power of the Spirit of God?

THE WHEAT AND THE TARES

Read Matthew 13:24–30 and answer the following.

To what does Jesus compare the kingdom of heaven? (v. 24)

What happens after the good seed is sown, and what does it cause? (vv. 25–26)

How long will the wheat and the tares live side by side? (v. 30)

What can we conclude about the kingdom's impact on society, as represented by the field? (v. 24)

Though the kingdom of God is already present, it is not yet consummated or concluded. Therefore God's people will live side by side with unredeemed people until the Age to Come. Furthermore, only God is fully capable of distinguishing children of the kingdom from children of the Evil One.

THE MUSTARD SEED AND THE LEAVEN

Read Matthew 13:31–33 and answer the following.

To what does Jesus now compare the kingdom of heaven? (vv. 31, 33)

Though the mustard seed is the least of all the seeds, what happens when it is grown? (v. 32) What happens when the leaven is hid? (v. 33)

Inasmuch as Jesus' main point is to state contrasts, what do we learn here about the kingdom of God now and the kingdom of God in its later, ultimate consummation?

The kingdom of God, present now in less-than-final form, will one day be great and completely victorious, sovereign without rivalry.

THE HIDDEN TREASURE AND THE PEARL

Read Matthew 13:44–46 and answer the following. To what two things does Jesus now compare the kingdom of heaven? (v. 44)

What does the man do when he finds the hidden treasure? (v. 44) the merchant when he finds the pearl? (v. 46)

What does Jesus appear to be teaching?

How is the kingdom of God of inestimable value; and why should a person do all that he can to receive it by faith and participate in its life?

THE DRAGNET

Read Matthew 13:47–50 and answer the following. In this seventh parable, to what does Jesus compare the kingdom of heaven? (v. 47)

What happens when the dragnet is cast into the sea? (vv. 47–48)

What is Jesus' point? (vv. 49–50)

In the Age to Come, God's kingdom will contain a sinless community. But for now, the invitation to God's reign is open to all. We are never to determine who is and who is not "fit" to hear the message of God's kingdom; this was one of the problems with the Pharisees that led to their eventual demise. Neither are we able to make the final determination as to who belongs to God and who does not.

THE GROWING SEED

Read Mark 4:26–29 and answer the following. To what does Jesus compare the kingdom of God? (v. 26)

What happens after the man scatters his seed? (vv. 27–28)

The next thing the man knows, what has happened? (v. 29)

What does Jesus' main point seem to be?

Jesus here teaches the supernatural nature of the kingdom of God and compares it to a seed growing in the ground.

 FAITH ALIVE

What has been especially new and/or convicting to you in this study?

Would you say you live your Christian life with a conscious awareness that the possibilities of God's powerful reign resides within you through the Holy Spirit?

How would you measure your receptivity to the truths of God's kingdom?

Assess these questions in prayer and listen to what the Holy Spirit might say to you.

1. Some people distinguish between "the kingdom of God" and "the kingdom of heaven," but parallel Synoptic passages show that these phrases mean the same thing. For example, Matthew 10:7 equals Luke 9:2, and Matthew 11:11 equals Luke 7:28. "Of God" is the more common designation, while "of heaven" is distinctive to Matthew, probably because "heaven" was an indirect way first-century Jews referred to God.
2. Joachim Jeremias, *New Testament Theology* (New York: Charles Scribner's Sons, 1971), 98. Used by permission.
3. Karl Schmidt, *Theological Dictionary of the New Testament*, Vol. 1 (Grand Rapids: Eerdmans, 1974), 589. Used by permission.
4. I. Howard Marshall, *Commentary on Luke* (Grand Rapids: Eerdmans, 1978), 184. Used by permission.
5. *Spirit-Filled Life Bible*, 1475, "Word Wealth: Mark 4:11 mystery."
6. Ibid., 1428–29, note on Matt. 13:3.

Lesson 4/The Kingdom of God Demonstrated

Of his ministry at Corinth Paul wrote, "My speech and my preaching were not with persuasive words of human wisdom, but in demonstration of the Spirit and of power, that your faith should not be in the wisdom of men but in the power of God" (1 Cor. 2:4–5). He undoubtedly learned this from Jesus, whose words could never be deemed the wisdom of men. And yet with the power His words contained, Jesus knew that God's kingdom rule could not be effectively offered to people by teaching alone. He knew He must demonstrate the power and authenticity of what He taught. So Matthew clearly states that "Jesus went about all Galilee, teaching in their synagogues, preaching the gospel of the kingdom, and healing all kinds of sickness and all kinds of disease among the people" (4:23).

Modern western man may balk at the mention of miracles and works of power, but they are an integral part of Jesus' ministry, as well as in parts of the church today. A look at Jesus' life would be incomplete without examining some of His miracles and their impact on those who received them. Christ's miracles impact nature, human beings, and even the spirit world. They also accomplish some amount of redemption over the effects of the Fall and sin.

CLASSIFICATIONS

In Acts 2:22 Peter uses three words to describe Jesus' demonstrations of God's kingdom power. What are those words?

With the word "attested," Acts 2:22 explains why God performed such works of power through Jesus. What is the specific identity of Jesus to which these mighty works attest? (2:21–24; 32–36)

 WORD WEALTH

Miracle, *dunamis*; energy, power, might, great force, great ability, strength . . . the powers of the world to come at work upon the Earth . . . divine power overcoming all resistance. (Compare "dynamic," "dynamite," and "dynamometer.") The *dunamis* in Jesus resulted in dramatic transformations.[1]

Wonders, *teras; teras* denotes extraordinary occurrences, supernatural prodigies, omens, portents, unusual manifestations, miraculous incidents portending the future rather than the past, and acts that are so unusual they cause the observer to marvel or be in awe.[2]

Signs, *semeion*; a sign, mark, token. Harrison explains that "'sign' points to a spiritual truth of which the miracle is the outward expression . . . [*semeion*] is the most important [description of a miracle] in relation to Jesus' mission. In its aspect as a sign, a miracle was a kind of acted parable, whose value lay in its correspondence with the spiritual lesson it was intended to convey."[3]

Miraculous demonstrations of the kingdom were expected of the Messiah (John 7:31). Jesus seems to have no problem with this expectation, except when people use miracles/wonders/signs for self-serving ends (study John 6 to see how He resists this). Let's take a moment now to examine some of the who, what, when, where, why, and how of Jesus' messianic deeds of power.

Read the following scriptures and note who receives a deed of power from Jesus and what their need is.

Matt. 8:28–34

Matt. 17:14–21

Mark 1:40–45

Mark 4:35–41

Luke 7:11–17

As Michael Green has written, "It would have been no good Jesus *talking* about the kingdom of God if He did not *do* anything about it. He did not come simply to proclaim the kingly rule of God but to bring it to bear directly on our everyday lives. In a word, He came to bring healing to a broken world. That is what *salvation* means: God's wholeness, His rescue at every level of our need. That is what Jesus set about doing."[4]

Read the following and note when or where Jesus performs deeds of power.

Mark 3:1–6

Mark 7:56

Luke 4:38–39

Luke 13:10–17

What pattern can you see?

Read the following and note why Jesus performs deeds of power.

Matt. 11:20–24

Matt. 12:28–29

Matt. 14:14

Mark 2:1–12

📖 **BIBLE EXTRA**

"Jesus' miracles . . . are signs of God's kingly rule, the dawn of which Jesus announced in his proclamation (Matt. 4:23; 9:35; Mark 1:39; 6:6; Luke 4:14f., 44). Jesus' words and works are the beginning of the age of salvation. The casting out of demons signals God's invasion into the realm of Satan and its final annihilation (Matt. 12:29 par. Mark 3:27; Luke 11:21f.; Is. 49:24f.; Luke. 10:18; John 12:31; Rev. 20:1ff., 10); the raising of the dead announces that death will be forever done away with (1 Cor. 15:26; Rev. 21:4; Is. 25:8); the healing of the sick bears witness to the cessation of all suffering (Rev. 21:4); the miraculous provisions of food are fore-tokens of the end of all physical need (Rev. 7:16f.); the stilling of the storm points forward to complete victory over the powers of chaos which threaten the earth (Rev. 21:1)."[5]

Read the following and note how Jesus performed deeds of power.

Matt. 8:1–4

Mark 7:31–37

Mark 8:22–26

Luke 8:49–56

BEHIND THE SCENES

In the ancient world, saliva supposedly had a healing function. The New Testament is silent, however, as to why Jesus used it on occasion as part of His healings. The best answer seems to be that its use "was simply an acted parable, to draw . . . attention to what Jesus was about to do."[6]

Also unique to the healing at Bethsaida is the fact that it is not instantaneous. (The only other close parallel is John 9, where after making saliva and spreading mud on the blind man's eyes, Jesus tells him to "Go, wash in the pool of Siloam" [John 9:7].) Mark gives no hint as to why this healing comes in stages. Calvin wrote: "He did so most probably for the purpose of proving, in the case of this man, that he had full liberty as to his method of proceeding, and was not restricted to a fixed rule. And so the grace of Christ, which had formerly been poured out suddenly on others, flowed by drops, as it were, on this man."[7]

THE PEOPLE'S RESPONSE

Jesus refused to perform miracles to rescue Himself (Luke 4:1–4; Matt. 26:51–54; 27:39–44). They were for the benefit of others, which is why His miracles are acts of mercy. Undoubtedly, great gratitude arose in the hearts of the recipients, but responses were often quite varied among non-recipients. These other responses stand out when we remember they were in effect a response to God visiting His people (Luke 7:16).

What is the response in Capernaum when Jesus cast the spirit out of the man in the synagogue? (Mark 1:21–28)

What is the response in Capernaum when He heals a paralytic man? (Mark 2:1–12)

What is the response of His disciples when Jesus stills the storm? (Mark 4:35–41)

What is the response of the Gadarenes when Jesus casts a legion of spirits out of a demon-possessed man? (Mark 5:1–20)

What is the general response of those in Nazareth to Jesus' mighty works? (Mark 6:1–6)

The gospel writers make it clear that miracles have a limited effect in producing *lasting* faith in Jesus Christ. As we shall see in the next chapter, miracles can even create such opposition that people may conclude that Jesus is in league with Satan (Matt. 12:24). For miracles to be truly understood, they must be tied in to discipleship, which is why Jesus does not want to be known merely as a miracle worker (Mark 8:26) and why the sin issue is often addressed along with a miracle.

MIRACLES AND DISCIPLESHIP

Both Jesus (Mark 1:14–15) and John the Baptist (Matt. 3:2) associate the presence of the kingdom of God with repentance. God's kingdom rule through Jesus Christ brings new birth, character growth, and miraculous dominion over effects of the Fall (see Luke 10:17–20). So it is, as Paul reminds the Corinthians (1 Cor. 12—14), that the fruit and power of the Holy Spirit must be linked to kingdom ministry.

Read Mark 2:1–12 and note how Jesus ties together the miracle of healing and discipleship.

What is the key to the paralytic's healing? (v. 5)

What does Jesus address first in the man's life? (v. 5)

What is Jesus ultimately establishing through this healing? (v. 10)

"Son, your sins are forgiven you" (v. 5) reinforces the close relationship the Bible declares to exist between sin and sickness (James 5:15–16). It also reinforces Jesus' concern that we remember that God's reign is here to bring wholeness to our entire person.

RELEASING THE DEMONIZED

Of Christ's miracles, exorcisms are the most frequent. Perhaps more than other types of miracles, they graphically illustrate that the kingdom of God is overthrowing Satan's kingdom. Jesus Himself says, "If I cast out demons by the Spirit of God, surely the kingdom of God has come upon you" (Matt. 12:28). In the New Testament, demons are on occasion linked with blindness and muteness (Matt. 12:22), deafness (Mark 9:25), deformity of the body (Luke 13:10–17), mental problems (Matt. 8:28), and even social dysfunction (Luke 8:27, 35).

THE DEMONIAC OF GADARENE

Of all Jesus' exorcisms, that of the man from Gadarene is perhaps most intriguing, not only because he is possessed by many demons but because the demons bicker with Jesus. Read Mark 5:1–20 and note the following.

The unclean spirit has reduced the man to living where? (v. 3)

What effects does the unclean spirit have on him? (vv. 3–5)

What does Jesus first say to him? (v. 8)

What response does this produce?[8] (vv. 6–7)

Mark's explanation in verse 8 as to why the man "cried out with a loud voice" is somewhat surprising. We have no other New Testament record of demons initially resisting Jesus. "It is implied that the demon was not compelled to obey Jesus at once."[9] Though we must be careful what we conclude from this, at least we can see that exorcisms may require time and effort (Mark 9:14–29).

What does Jesus next ask the man? What do we learn from his answer? (v. 9)

Jesus asks the demon its name because He may be demanding its submission thereby. "My name is Legion," reflects the degree of the man's bondage to a multitude of evil spirits. (A Roman legion numbered 3,000 to 6,000 men.)

What is the unclean spirits' request (v. 12) and how does Jesus respond to it? (v. 13)

We cannot be certain why Jesus made this concession, but what does seem clear is that the fate of the swine illustrates the fate the unclean spirits intended for the man. It certainly sobers the townsfolk! (v. 15)

What is the state of the man following his encounter with God's kingdom reign? (v. 15)

 FAITH ALIVE

Read Mark 9:14–29. In this passage Jesus Christ gives three kingdom keys to commanding an evil spirit to leave.

In Mark 9:19 for what does Jesus rebuke His disciples? and how did this affect God's power?

Jesus Christ reveals the first kingdom key in verse 9. What is it?

In verse 29 Jesus Christ outlines the other two keys by taking authority over this deaf and dumb spirit. What are they?

Finally, what is the importance of fasting in releasing spiritual power?

Regarding this passage, whether or not you will ever need to cast out an evil spirit, which of these three kingdom keys do you need to better learn to use? Why?

1. *Spirit-Filled Life Bible*, 1632, "Word Wealth: Acts 4:33 power."
2. Ibid., 1655, "Word Wealth: Acts 15:12 wonders."
3. Everett Harrison, *A Short Life of Christ* (Grand Rapids: Eerdmans, 1977), 112.
4. Michael Green, *Who Is This Jesus?* (Nashville: Thomas Nelson, 1992), 39.
5. Colin Brown, ed., *Dictionary of New Testament Theology*, Vol. 2 (Grand Rapids: Zondervan, 1979), 631. Used by permission.
6. R. Alan Cole, *Tyndale New Testament Commentaries: Mark* (Grand Rapids: Eerdmans, 1989), 200.
7. Frank E. Gaebelein, ed., *The Expositor's Bible Commentary*, Vol. 8 (Grand Rapids: Zondervan, 1984), 691.
8. "What have I to do with You?" (v. 7) corresponds to "Why do You interfere with me?" It may also mean a threat like, "Mind Your own business!"
9. C.E.B. Cranfield, *The Gospel According To St. Mark* (Cambridge: Cambridge University Press, 1974), 178. Used by permission.

Lesson 5/Resistance and Confusion

Have you ever known someone who was too proud or stubborn to receive a gift from you? How about someone so set in his ways that he resisted ever attempting something new? Have you ever been surprised or confused over someone's behavior because it was not what you expected?

These questions reflect some responses to Jesus' life and ministry. As we have established, Jesus did not come to Israel according to *her* messianic expectations. He came to radically reshape people's thinking. Some humbled themselves and rose to the occasion; "Blessed are the poor in spirit, for theirs is the kingdom of heaven" (Matt. 5:3). Others were only superficial in their response, not surviving the long haul (Matt. 13:20–21; Luke 9:57–58). Still others, especially among the Pharisees and religious leaders, resisted so vehemently Jesus once said, "Woe to you, scribes and Pharisees, hypocrites! For you shut up the kingdom of heaven against men; for you neither go in *yourselves*, nor do you allow those who are entering to go in" (Matt. 23:13). Notice that their resistance not only closed the door for themselves; it also "shut up" the kingdom of heaven to others as well. As teachers of the Old Testament, they should have been opening up the kingdom of God to their disciples.

In this chapter we want to examine two important realities taught in the Synoptics: the Pharisaic resistance and the genuine confusion that arose among Jesus' disciples. The nature of the disciples' confusion is important because it illustrates our bewilderment when God does not do things our way. The nature of the Pharisees' resistance is important, because, even though the New Testament clearly teaches that the Cross is God's redemptive plan (Acts 2:22–23), the

Gospels also portray satanically backed pharisaical resistance as pivotal in putting Jesus on the cross (Luke 22:3–6; 23:34).

🚪 BEHIND THE SCENES

Pharisee means "separated one." They descended from the second century B.C. Hasidim, a pious Jewish sect who insisted on strictly observing the Jewish ritual laws at a time when many Jews were compromising under Roman and Hellenistic (Grecian world) influence. They soon gained favor with Roman and Greek leadership and were granted representation on Israel's legislative body, the Sanhedrin.

"One distinctive feature of the Pharisees was their strong commitment to observing the law of God as it was interpreted and applied by the scribes. The way in which the scribes spelled out the meaning of the Mosaic Law, the ways in which they adapted that Law to suit the needs of their day, the time-honored customs which they endorsed—all these became a part of the 'tradition of the elders' (Mark 7:3). . . . the Pharisees . . . were known for supporting and keeping the 'tradition of the elders' . . . especially . . . the laws of tithing and ritual purity."[1]

At the time of Jesus, they were mostly laymen organized into brotherhoods. Inasmuch as the Sadducees controlled the temple priesthood, the Pharisees operated the local synagogues and were backed by the Sanhedrin, over which they exerted a strong influence (Acts 5:34–40; 23:6–10).

PHARISAIC OBJECTIONS

Many of Israel's rank and file "were astonished at His teaching, for [Jesus] taught them as one having authority, and not as the scribes" (Mark 1:22). But the Pharisees were not so impressed, especially since "public opinion," i.e., Jesus, was criticizing their heroes. They took issue with Jesus from the start because He had not been trained in either the Pharisaic school of Hillel or Shammai.[2]

What was their point of contention over Jesus' dealings with the paralyzed man? (Luke 5:17–21)

What was their contention in Mark 2:16?

The Pharisees felt it was more important to avoid potential ceremonial defilement than to help those in need.

According to Luke 5:33 and Mark 7:1–5, the Pharisees say that Jesus does not have enough regard for what two important disciplines of their tradition?

The command to wash their hands (Mark 7:3) is from the tradition later called the Mishnah, a written tradition of the elders, not the Mosaic Law. This ordinance involved washing their hands in a special way, although we cannot be sure exactly what that special way was.

One of the Pharisees' greatest contentions is their perception of Jesus' attitude toward the Law in general. What is their accusation? (Matt. 5:17)

According to Matthew 12:1–8 and Luke 6:6–11, they accuse Him of having disregard for what else?

What is their contention in Matthew 26:61? John tells us that because of their spiritual blindness they fail to perceive what? (John 2:19–22)

Although it is not recorded in the Synoptics, John 5:16–18 records a crowning offense to the Pharisees. What is it?

PHARISAIC TACTICS

The Pharisees hound Jesus even in semi-private settings (see Mark 2:24). "They watched Him closely . . . so that they might accuse Him" (Mark 3:2). "Watched closely" (Greek, *paratereo*) has the idea of lying in wait to catch someone in an act of transgression. This mood of criticism prompts public questions aimed at undermining Jesus' credibility as a spiritual leader (Mark 2:16; 7:5). Read the following verses and note the tactics.

Matt. 16:1

Matt. 22:15–17, Mark 10:2

Mark 3:6

Matt. 26:14–16

PHARISAIC SLANDER

The Pharisees' accusations come to a head in Matthew 12:22–37 when Jesus heals a demon-possessed, blind, and mute man.

What is the reaction of the multitudes to this healing? (v. 23)

What is the reaction of the Pharisees? (v. 24)

Jesus notes that their accusation is illogical by pointing out what? (vv. 25–26)

Here "Beelzebub, the ruler of the demons" is a synonym for Satan. The derivation of this name is uncertain. Scholarly guesses range from "lord of flies" (a variation of Baal-Zebub, the god of Ekron [2 Kin. 1:2]) to "lord of dung" or "lord of the heights/heaven."

What does this healing clearly indicate? (vv. 28–29)

The Pharisees' accusation is actually against whom? (v. 31)

The Pharisees' charge is that of satanic sorcery, a capital offense in the Mishnah, an interpretive commentary the Pharisees used. Mark reports an even stronger, additional charge, "He has Beelzebub" (3:22).

What is the consequence of this accusation? (v. 32)

Robert Guelich explains that "Jesus' opponents were attributing to Satan God's redemptive activity in Jesus through the work of the Spirit. In so doing, they not only were rejecting Jesus but also God's offer of redemptive activity in history. One commits the 'unpardonable sin,' therefore, by rejecting God's redemptive overture for humanity in Jesus Christ."[3]

JESUS' REACTIONS

In spite of their tactics, Jesus is not implacably hostile toward these Pharisees. On occasion He dines with them (Luke 7:36) and is willing to discuss spiritual matters with those who will listen (John 3:1–21). However, as seen in Jesus' interchange in Matthew 12, He solidly resists the Pharisees when necessary. For example, their accusation that His deliverance ministry is blasphemy *against* the Spirit (12:31) comes back on them (John 5:18).

Read the following scriptures and note Jesus' charge against them.

Matt. 23:4

Matt. 23:5–7

Matt. 23:13–15

Matt. 23:16–22

Matt. 23:23–24

Mark 7:9–13

What is Jesus' overall summation of their problem? (Matt. 22:29) What is a major root cause of this problem? (Luke 18:9)

   WORD WEALTH

Hypocrite, *hupokrites.* In the New Testament, this word is a regular expression for wicked and godless people. They are such because they reject the truth about God's kingdom in Jesus, not out of ignorance but willful blindness. Their hypocrisy involves deliberate pretense with a clear knowledge of the truth (see Mark 7:6–13). Their hypocrisy is heightened because they feel no one can see as clearly as they do.

AT A GLANCE

Characteristics of Pharisaism
The following is a list of attitudes behind Pharisaism as Jesus encountered it. This list is not intended to be exhaus-

tive, and duplicate references to the same attitude are not included.

1. Pharisaism is drawn to religious activity — Matthew 3:7.
2. It boasts in ancestral religious merit — Matthew 3:9.
3. It associates only with those considered religiously and morally of the same vein — Matthew 9:11.
4. It makes quick and often uninsightful religious judgments based on preconceived theological premises — Matthew 9:33, 34.
5. It focuses on religious traditions more than people's extenuating circumstances and expresses no flexibility in bending amoral religious traditions to meet people's needs — Matthew 12:1–8.
6. It focuses on traditions more than people's healings — Matthew 12:9–14.
7. It focuses on religious tradition more than God's Word (Matthew 15:3–6), often to the setting aside of God's Word for tradition's sake — Mark 7:8–13.
8. It emphasizes outward appearance more than heart attitude — Matthew 15:7–9.
9. It always tests (with a negative attitude) the workings of God — Matthew 16:1.
10. It plans crafty plots aimed at trapping God's ministers — Matthew 22:15.
11. It does not live up to the truths it knows — Matthew 23:3.
12. It binds heavy religious burdens on people — Matthew 23:4.
13. It interests itself in men's praise — Matthew 23:5.
14. It glories in authoritative, hierarchical religious positions — Matthew 23: 6, 8.
15. It glories in authoritative titles — Matthew 23:7.
16. It glories in attention — Mark 12:38.
17. It has a way of preventing others from experiencing the things of God — Matthew 23:13.

 FAITH ALIVE

After reviewing the characteristics of Pharisaism, it is clear that the judgmental spirit of the Pharisee did not depart with the first century. Although there is a legitimate need for orthodoxy and scriptural purity, many in our day have adopted the role of the Pharisee by pronouncing judgment on legitimate ministers of God. Like the Pharisees of the New Testament, they are falsely accusing ministers of heresy.

Read Mark 3:20–22. What accusation did the Pharisees make about Jesus?

How does the Pharisees' accusation of Jesus in verse 22 relate to those who accuse legitimate ministers and ministries of being satanically inspired?

Why should we be very careful about making an accusation about a minister of Jesus Christ?

How can we be sure that we do not go beyond what the Word of God says but maintain balanced lives? (2 Tim. 2:15)

CONFUSED DISCIPLES

Though not intentionally resistant, even Jesus' most committed followers may be resistant at times due to a lack of understanding. James' and John's request for power and status (Mark 10:35–40) reflects their misunderstanding that Jesus is the Messiah who will *in the future* restore the glory of the throne of David to Israel. Jesus' response, "You do not know what you ask" (v. 38), addresses this misconception, and they also missed the truth that entering into His glory requires great suffering. Their confusion over His warning to "take heed and beware of the leaven of the Pharisees and the Sadducees" (Matt. 16:6) brings the response, "Do you not yet understand?" (v. 9). Even after his revelatory statement, "You are the Christ, the Son of the living God" (Matt. 16:16), Peter misunderstands Jesus' death and resurrection (Matt. 16:21–22)!

Perhaps the most unlikely confusion is that of John the Baptist. Borne out of disillusionment, John's confusion offers Jesus an opportunity to reinforce John's understanding of His messianic mission. Carefully read Matthew 11:2–15 and answer the following.

What is John's concern? (v. 3)

What prompts his concern? (v. 2)

Some have interpreted John's question as a loss of confidence in his mission because he's imprisoned. This is unlikely, however, because of Jesus' commendation (v. 9) and His statement that John is anything but weak and vacillating (v. 7).

What is Jesus' response? (vv. 4–5) How does it compare with Luke 4:16–21?[4]

What does Jesus realize about the nature of His ministry? (Matt. 11:6)

Scholar Donald Hagner correctly notes that Matthew 11:5 "is in complete accord with Matthew's stress on Jesus and his ministry as the fulfillment of the Old Testament promises. There is in Jesus' concluding words, however, an indirect admission that not everything will work out in accord with John's expectations. If Jesus is the Messiah, he is not the kind of Messiah awaited by John and the populace at large. In short, John is meant to understand that he was correct in his recognition of Jesus as the promised one but that he must also be prepared to accept the fact that the kingdom Jesus brings does not, for the time being anyway, entail the judgment of the wicked. Indeed, on the contrary, the message of the kingdom goes precisely to the unrighteous (see 9:13)."[5]

To whom does Jesus now turn His attention (v. 7) and what does He ask? (vv. 7–9)

John's preaching created quite a stir, with remarkable response (Matt. 3:1–12). Jesus now examines the people's motives to show that John's ministry has significance only in relation to His messianic mission. Jesus' rhetorical questions build to suggest motives progressively closer to understanding John's ministry. "A reed shaken by the wind" (v. 7), for example, metaphorically suggests someone who is weak and vacillating, which obviously John is not.

What is John's assignment and what is Jesus' assessment of him? (vv. 9–11)

John's position and role at the turning point of redemptive history make him the most important of all the Old Testament figures; but no Old Testament ministry can compare to ministry in the church age, no matter how "insignificant" that ministry might seem (v. 11).

What is the nature of the kingdom of heaven in which we participate? (v. 12)

English translators vary on how to render the Greek verb *biazetai* in verse 12. Some translate it, "suffers violence." Others translate it, "has been coming violently." The latter is probably best. Jesus' messianic mission has set up a powerful movement that penetrates human history and overthrows the satanic kingdom with God's mighty power, even violence.

What kind of people lay hold of this advancing kingdom, and with what attitude? (v. 12)

"The violent" are keenly enthusiastic disciples who wholeheartedly respond to God's reign; they make radical decisions and rigorous commitments (see Mark 9:43, 47; Luke 14:33). Luke's version reads, "The law and the prophets were until John. Since that time the kingdom of God has been preached, and everyone is pressing into it" (16:16).

Pastor Jack Hayford explains how notions of violence and pressing in pertain to God's saving rule on earth: "Jesus declares the advance of the kingdom of God is the result of two things: preaching and pressing in. He shows the gospel of the kingdom must be proclaimed with spiritual passion. In every generation believers have to determine whether they will respond to this truth with sensible minds and sensitive hearts. To overlook it will bring a passivity that limits the ministry of God's kingdom [merely] to extending the terms of truth and love—that is, teaching or educating and engaging in acts of kindness. Without question, we must do these things. However, apart from 1) an impassioned pursuit of prayer, 2) confrontation with the demonic, 3) expectation of the miraculous, and 4) a burning heart for evangelism, the kingdom of God makes little penetration in the world.

"At the same time, overstatement of 'pressing' is likely to produce rabid fanatics who justify any behavior in Jesus' name as applying the boldness spoken of here. Such travesties in church history as the Crusades and various efforts at politicizing in a quest to produce righteousness in society through Earth-level rule are extremes we must learn to reject. 'Pressing in' is accomplished first in prayer warfare, coupled with a will to surrender one's life and self-interests, in order to gain God's kingdom goal."[6]

In verse 10, Jesus (quoting Mal. 3:1) identifies John again as the forerunner of the Messiah. In verse 14, Jesus outright identifies John as coming in the same ministry capacity as who?

This does not mean John is literally a revived or reincarnated Elijah, a claim John himself denies (John 1:21); rather that he functions in the spirit of Elijah as prophesied in Malachi 4:5.

 FAITH ALIVE

Are you willing to be a "violent" disciple? Do you live the Christian life aggressively? Are you perhaps over-pressing, causing those around you to be more repelled than attracted by the gospel? Do you passionately pursue prayer? Have you been trained to understand spiritual warfare and confrontation with the demonic? Do you live with an expectation of the miraculous and a passion for evangelism? Assess these questions in prayer before the Lord with a contrite spirit, willing to be encouraged or corrected as He sees fit. Also, as you have opportunity, share your findings with others as a point of prayer and accountability.

1. *Nelson's Illustrated Bible Dictionary*, 830.
2. Two leading rabbis during Jesus' day; Hillel promoted a more liberal interpretation of the Law than did Shammai, who was more strict. The former's was the more widely accepted view.
3. Robert Guelich, *Word Biblical Commentary: Mark* (Dallas: Word, 1989), 185.
4. See Lesson 3, "God's Kingdom in the New Testament," for the significance of Jesus' response.
5. Donald A. Hagner, *Word Biblical Commentary: Matthew* (Dallas: Word, 1993), 301.
6. *Spirit-Filled Life Bible*, 1547, "Kingdom Dynamics: Luke 16:16, 'Pressing in,' Conflict and the Kingdom."

Lesson 6/Who Are These Disciples?

The most important work of Christ before His death and resurrection was the selection and training of the men who would represent Him in the world in the coming days. To these men He devoted himself almost exclusively in the interval between the resurrection and the ascension, and very largely so in the months prior to His death.

Luke records in Acts 4:13 that "when [the Sanhedrin] saw the boldness of Peter and John, and perceived that they were uneducated and untrained men, they marveled. And they realized that they had been with Jesus." The Sanhedrin were miffed that these laymen ("uneducated and untrained") had no formal training in any rabbinical school and that their only credentials were that they had been with Jesus, who Himself seems not to have studied formally (John 7:15). And yet the ruling Jews could not help but marvel at the insight and spiritual power of both Jesus and his disciples.

As if to reinforce this, John writes, "Most assuredly, I say to you, he who believes in Me, the works that I do he will do also; and greater works than these will he do, because I go to My Father" (14:12).

Who are these followers? Why does He choose them? How does He choose and train them? What is their commission? What is their relationship to us, the modern church? Is it fair to look at their lives as models of reproducible ministry?

These are some of the questions we'll wrestle with in this chapter. We want to understand the call, conversion, and commission of His closest disciples and examine to what degree they are prototypes of Christian ministries. Turning tax-collectors and fishermen into devoted followers of the Way is exciting, especially when we realize that Jesus is still patiently doing the same today.

WORD WEALTH

Disciple, *mathetes,* comes "from the verb *manthano,* 'to learn,' whose root *math* suggests thought with effort put forth. A disciple is a learner, one who follows both the teaching and the teacher. The word is used first of the Twelve and later of Christians generally."[1] It basically describes any convert to Christianity, as well as those truly devoted to pressing in to His life.

BEHIND THE SCENES

Jesus' relationship to His disciples begins differently than the norm in His culture. Typically, a student would seek out a rabbi under whose tutelage he then submitted. This is probably how John's disciples followed him. In the case of Jesus, however, He takes the initiative. "Follow Me, and I will make you become fishers of men" (Mark 1:17). "You did not choose Me, but I chose you" (John 15:16). This is why the most common designation in the synoptic Gospels for those aligned with Jesus is not simply "the disciples," but "His disciples."

THE TWELVE

"The Twelve" is one of the special names for the group of men Jesus selected as His original apostles (Mark 4:10; Luke 6:13). Matthew referred to them as "His twelve disciples" (10:1). With the exception of Judas Iscariot, a Judean, they are all Galileans, like their Master. The number twelve is significant to the twelve tribes of Israel (Matt. 19:28).

What are their names? (Luke 6:14–16)

Among the Twelve are two named Simon. What is the political affiliation of the second Simon? (Luke 6:15)

Mark (3:18) and Matthew (10:4) call him "Simon the Cananite," but this does not mean he is from Cana or Canaan.

"Cananite," here, is a Greek transliteration of the Aramaic word for Zealot, which explains why Luke called Simon "the Zealot."

What additional name does Jesus later give to John? (Mark 3:17)

As was common among first-century Jews, "Judas *the son* of James" (Luke 6:16) has a second name. What is it? (Mark 3:18)

Matthew also has another name. What is it? (Mark 2:14) What is his occupation when called? (Matt. 10:2)

"Tax collector" here likely refers to a customs official who sat in a roadside toll booth to collect customs or transport taxes for Herod Antipas. Jewish tax collectors were considered unpatriotic, and they were despised for their regular contact with the ritually unclean.

Who among the Twelve are brothers? (Matt. 10:2)

What is one of Jesus' primary reasons for calling disciples? (Matt. 4:19)

During His final Passover meal with the Twelve, Luke records Jesus' affectionate words of appreciation to His loyal group (22:28–30).

For what does He commend them? (v. 28)

What does He confer on them? (v. 29)

What does He promise them? (v. 30)

They will be with Him and somehow participate in His ultimate messianic rulership. Matthias will apparently occupy the place of Judas Iscariot in the fulfillment of this promise (Acts 1:15–26).

BEHIND THE SCENES

The Twelve Apostles[2]

The 12 apostles are listed in Matthew 10:2–4; Mark 3:14–19; Luke 6:13–16; and Acts 1:13. Each list divides into three groups of four apostles each (see below). The first group consists of two pairs of brothers—Simon Peter and Andrew, James and John—who had been fishermen (Matt. 4:18–22). Philip, Bartholomew, Thomas, and Matthew make up the second group. Matthew, the tax collector, was also known as Levi (see Matt. 9:9; Luke 5:27).

Names vary in the third group. All of the lists include James son of Alphaeus and Judas Iscariot. But Matthew and Mark refer to Thaddaeus (surname of Lebbaeus) and Simon the Cananite while Luke and Acts list Judas the son of James and Simon the Zealot. Judas the son of James and Thaddaeus were probably the same person. He may have been called Judas Thaddaeus. If so, Thaddaeus would have served to distinguish him from Judas Iscariot (see Matt. 10:3). Simon the Cananite and Simon the Zealot were undoubtedly the same person. Cananite should probably be understood as Cananaean. Cananaean is the Aramaic word for Zealot.

Simon (Peter)	Philip	James (son of Alphaeus)
Andrew	Bartholomew	Judas Iscariot
James (son of Zebedee)	Thomas	Thaddaeus (Lebbaeus, Judas)
John	Matthew (Levi)	Simon (the Cananite, the Zealot)

THEIR TRAINING

Jesus' initial call on their lives is to follow Him. In so doing, He will model kingdom life, character, and ministry for them. He will confront their characters, challenge their priorities, teach them, rebuke them, empower them, commission them and ultimately entrust them to continue doing what He "began both to do and teach" (Acts 1:1). All this occurs in about three years' time.

According to Matthew 5:1—7:29, what is one way in which He educates them?

According to Matt. 13:10–11, what is another method He uses?

According to Mark 6:45–52, what is one way He teaches them to trust in God amidst adverse conditions?

Before commissioning them to ministry on their own, what is one way Jesus initiates them into ministering the miraculous? (Mark 6:30–44)

Realizing that we sometimes learn valuable character lessons through direct confrontation, the Master occasionally confronts sin and deficiency in the lives of the Twelve. Read the following scriptures and note what character deficiency He addresses or what character trait He wants to see develop.

Luke 9:49–50

Luke 9:51–56

A testimony to John's obedience and God's grace is that some years later Luke notes John "prayed for [the Samaritans] that they might receive the Holy Spirit" (Acts 8:15).

Mark 10:35–45

Jesus desires that we serve Him as grateful, humble servants, not that we come to Him seeking opportunities for personal advancement. So important is this, and so difficult for the human ego to grasp, that Jesus demonstrates it again during His final Passover meal (John 13:1–20). What does the Master demonstrate?

An integral part of their training is the ongoing challenge to their priorities and instructions about the requirements of biblical discipleship.

How does Luke summarize the conditions of discipleship? (14:26–27, 33)

This being the case, what does Jesus instruct would-be disciples to do? (Luke 14:28–32)

 PROBING THE DEPTHS

Biblical discipleship is costly (Luke 14:25–33). Having come *to* Jesus, one must then *follow* Him. "Hate" (v. 26) is not against people; for Jesus instructs us to love even our enemies (Luke 6:27). The Greek verb here (*miseo*) is based on the Hebrew or Aramaic expression "to love less" or "to renounce" (in terms of primary allegiance). Jesus Christ and His purposes are to be our number one allegiance. His call to forsake all that [one] has (v. 33) reinforces this. His disciples must be ever ready to renounce whatever He may ask for the sake of the kingdom. It is not saying disciples cannot own things, nor is it saying we are to forsake responsibilities. Rather, we are to be controlled by Jesus' ongoing call on our lives, and not by things or circumstances.

What else can we learn about discipleship from Matt. 10:24–25?

What is the difference between "bearing one's cross" and resisting the devil? (James 4:7)

How can we discern the difference between "taking up our cross" (Matt. 10:38) and standing against the wiles of the devil? (Eph. 6:10–13)

THEIR COMMISSION

Having called and trained the Twelve, Jesus realizes the next step in their training is a commissioning. It is time they go out alone to do what they have heard and what they have seen Him do. Read Matthew 10:1–15 and note the following.

What does Jesus give them to fulfill their commission? (v. 1)

 WORD WEALTH

Authority, *exousia.* The power, authority, and freedom to act which characterizes God. This same *exousia* resided in Jesus to complete His ministry, especially to disarm Satan's kingdom (Luke 4:36), to forgive sins, and to heal (Matt. 9:2–8). The Christian's *exousia* is delegated, finding its source in Christ's rulership over Satan, sin, and sickness. Christ's purpose in mediating His *exousia* to Christians is for kingdom service. Luke's account of the commissioning of the Twelve (10:1) indicates they also receive **power** (*dunamis*)— "energy, power, might, great force, great ability, strength. The *dunamis* in Jesus resulted in dramatic transformations. This is the norm for the Spirit-filled and Spirit-led church."[3]

To whom are they to minister? (v. 6)

What is the primary purpose of their commissioning? (v. 7)

This is the same message preached by both John the Baptist (Matt. 3:2) and Jesus (Matt. 4:17).

What is to attend their proclamation? (v. 8)

The Twelve have seen Jesus do each of these things in conjunction with His preaching (Matt. 8:3; 8:15; 8:32; 9:25). Again, these demonstrations are both acts of mercy and signs of God's kingly rule, which they are preaching—the "gospel of the kingdom." It is unlikely that this commission was understood or fulfilled any other way than literally; however, by the time of Matthew's writing, the church probably understood these attendant demonstrations to be both literal and spiritual acts of power in people's lives. (See "God's Kingdom in the New Testament" in chapter 3 above for a further explanation of this twofold significance.)

The Twelve are not to profit from their mission (vv. 8–10), but what are they to receive? (v. 10)

How must they respond to a rejection of the message? (v. 14)

To "shake off the dust from [one's] feet" was an act of repudiation, indicating that those who rejected the kingdom message were viewed as pagan and liable to severe judgment (v. 15).

We began this chapter by asking, What is the disciples' relationship to the modern church? Is it correct to look at their lives as models of reproducible ministry? The answer to this best derives from two incidents in Luke.

One is found in Luke 12:32, where Jesus tells His disciples, "Do not fear, little flock, for it is your Father's good pleasure to give you the kingdom." "Little flock" is Old Testament terminology for God's current "fold." As such, they are the *nucleus* of God's new people, the church (see Matt. 16:18). Therefore, Jesus' commission to them in Matthew 10, as well as His promise in John 14:12 about continuing His works, are our commission and promise as well (see Matt. 28:16–20; Acts 1:1–2).

Luke solidifies this when Jesus later commissions seventy others. Read Luke 10:1–20 and note the following.

What is their twofold commission? (v. 9)

Matthew indicates that the Twelve are commissioned to preach the gospel with demonstrations of the kingdom attending that. Luke records the command to "heal the sick" before the command to preach. Demonstrations of the kingdom's presence are apparently seen by Jesus as avenues to open the door for preaching, as well as confirmations of the preached message (see Luke 11:20).

Why are they able to speak and do these things? (v. 16)

As with the Twelve (Matt. 10:1), the seventy are granted delegated authority (v. 19).

What do they encounter on their mission and what is their response? (v. 17)

What does Jesus indicate that this signifies? (v. 18)

Though proclamation and demonstration of the kingdom are exciting, Jesus warns them and us to not lose sight of God's ultimate priority. What is of paramount importance to God? (v. 20)

 FAITH ALIVE

Take time in prayer to consider these questions: Does your heart beat after truly committed discipleship? Can you honestly say Jesus and His kingdom are your number one priority? Do you have any interests that you favor more than His interests? How do you respond when He tests your loyalties? Do you see yourself as fulfilling the commission given the Twelve and the seventy? Do you pray that God will use you in these capacities throughout the routines of daily living?

In what way will you break the present hold of Satan over people's lives, and why is what you do in Jesus' name and power important?

1. *Spirit-Filled Life Bible* (Nashville: Thomas Nelson, 1991), 1421, "Word Wealth: Matt. 10:1 disciples."
2. *The Wesley Study Bible* (Nashville: Thomas Nelson Publishers, 1990), 1429.
3. *Spirit-Filled Life Bible*, 1632, "Word Wealth: Acts 4:33 power."

Lesson 7/But I Say to You

The English word "ethic" is derived from the Greek *ethos,* meaning character. It has to do with morals and moral principles and distinctions between what is right and wrong, with a means of determining the obligations we have one to another. Though the moral foundations for determining a society's ethic are greatly diverse today, with many pushing for ethics based on each individual's desires, society still maintains an ethical, moral, and legal framework. Although standards are largely humanistic, they nevertheless provide an ethical structure.

Yet in both the Old and New Testaments God introduces a radically different set of ethics through the Ten Commandments, Old Testament laws of social conduct, the New Testament lists of virtues, and the Sermon on the Mount (our topic for this chapter).

But with God, ethical definition alone is not enough, for Christ brings a dynamic as well. Realizing the power of Satan and the strength of our fallen nature (sinful), He who defines also graciously enables us by his power. "His divine power has given to us all things that *pertain* to life and godliness, through the knowledge of Him who called us by glory and virtue" (2 Peter 1:3).

As we examine the Sermon on the Mount, please note: its call is to the *already converted*; for those in whom the reign of God—or kingdom—has begun. Apart from the Spirit's indwelling through a personal relationship with Jesus Christ, the ethical standards in Matthew 5—7 become impossible legal demands, bringing only increased frustration, defeat, and shame. As George Eldon Ladd explains, "The Sermon is not law. It portrays the ideal of the man in whose life the reign of God is absolutely realized. It can . . . to a real degree be attained in the present age, insofar as the reign of God is actually experienced."[1]

With these perspectives in mind, let's explore this very exciting "manifesto of kingdom life." But be forewarned. It is not only exciting, but humbling. In addition to listing several duties and dangers involved in being a disciple, it calls for a righteousness of heart and emphasizes inner character that manifests itself in outward conduct.

JESUS AND THE LAW

Because the Sermon stands in a tradition of the LORD God's definition of ethics for His people, Jesus references the Old Testament law on several occasions (5:21, 27, 31, 33, and so on). The Sermon cannot be understood apart from Jesus' understanding and fulfillment of the Old Testament. Read Matthew 5:17–20 and note the following.

Because Jesus' interpretation of the Law is so different from that of the Pharisees and religious leaders of His day, what do many Jews apparently think Jesus is doing? (v. 17)

What has He come to do with the Law and the Prophets? (v. 17)

"The Law [and] the Prophets" is a broad expression for the entire Old Testament (Matt. 11:13), the Law referring specifically to the Mosaic law code sections in the Pentateuch. "He came to fulfill the Old Testament in the sense of bringing to completion its partial revelation, in bringing to pass its messianic predictions, and in giving the true interpretation to its moral precepts."[2] In so doing, Jesus will state that some of the Law has fulfilled its role and is no longer applicable (Mark 7:17–23).

Jesus reiterates His commitment to fulfill the Law by stating what? (v. 18)

WORD WEALTH

Jot (Greek, *iota*) is the smallest letter of the Greek alphabet, used in Matthew 5:18 to refer to the smallest Hebrew letter, the *yod*. **Tittle** (Greek, *kepaia*) refers to the ornamental markings often added to the Hebrew text. Jesus emphatically drives home His point that the Law will be around until "all is fulfilled" (v. 18).

Jesus sees a negative and positive response to His understanding of God's commandments. What are they? (v. 19)

Jesus' reference is to levels of commitment among believers. Depth of discipleship has a direct bearing on depth of obedience and depth of desire to instruct others in His ways.

Getting to the heart of the matter, how does Jesus sum up what He has been saying? (v. 20)

 ## FAITH ALIVE

Before proceeding to look at the particulars in this new dimension of godliness Jesus presents, do you truly believe Peter's statement (2 Peter 1:3) that as a Christian you *can* live out God's ethical demands? Do you tend to read the Sermon on the Mount with anticipation of what you can increasingly become in thought and conduct, or with a sense of dread and anticipated failure? When holding these standards before others, do you tend to be harsh and point the finger, or to compassionately encourage, realizing that they are fulfilled only as one matures in his or her walk in the Spirit (Gal. 5:16)? Think and pray about these things before continuing.

THE BEATITUDES

Matthew 5:1 tells us that the Sermon takes place on a mountain, probably the steeply rising ground west of the Sea of

Galilee. Jesus has gone there hoping to escape the multitudes who are pressing on Him to be healed (4:25). When His disciples find Him, He uses the opportunity to teach them (5:2).

He begins with nine Beatitudes, declarations of blessing for those who have entered the kingdom of God and its ethical life. After identifying who is said to be blessed, each beatitude gives the reason or basis for being blessed.

 WORD WEALTH

Blessed, *makarios,* represents the Hebrew *'ashre*—fortunate, successful, or contented. As Donald Hagner explains, it "describes the nearly incomprehensible happiness of those who participate in the kingdom announced by Jesus. Rather than happiness in its mundane sense, it refers to the deep inner joy of those who have long awaited the salvation promised by God and who now begin to experience its fulfillment. The *makarioi* are the deeply or supremely happy."[3]

Read Matt. 5:3–12.

List the nine categories of those who are blessed (vv. 3–11).

   1.

   2.

   3.

   4.

   5.

   6.

   7.

   8.

   9.

List why each is blessed (vv. 3–11).

   1.

   2.

   3.

   4.

   5.

6.

7.

8.

9.

The ninth beatitude concludes with a parenthetical expansion that puts persecution into a larger framework. What is that framework? (v. 12)

 AT A GLANCE

Because of the familiarity of the Beatitudes, their richness sometimes escapes us. This chart states the essence of each beatitude and the key problem it addresses, and paraphrases each "backwards" so we can see what Jesus is teaching us *not* to be.

Beatitude's Essence	Overcome This Key Problem	In Other Words, Stated "Backwards"
#1—Have a receptive heart	Pride/rebellion	Miserable are the egocentric, self-sufficient and rebellious
#2—Stay tender-hearted, vulnerable to God and repentant	Self-righteousness/ insensitivity to conviction	Miserable are the unconvicted and emotionally indifferent
#3—Stay non-defensive, fully committed to God	Defensiveness/anger	Miserable are manipulators and those who insist on their own way
#4—Desire character development (sanctification)	Apathy/ false moral sophistication	Miserable are shallow disciples
#5—Treat others with the same grace God treats you	Ingratitude/ judgmentalism	Miserable are the judgmental and retaliatory
#6—Realize that character is the key to reality	Hypocrisy/ impure motives	Miserable are phonies who live secret lives
#7—Do your best to be in right relationship with God, others and yourself	Resentment/unresolved inner conflicts	Miserable are those who harbor any resentment or never put matters to rest

Beatitude's Essence	Overcome This Key Problem	In Other Words, Stated "Backwards"
#8—Realize that spiritual maturity calls for living under unjust pressure	Fear/insecurity	Miserable are those who compromise to avoid the pain of ethical growth
#9—Opt to learn God's redemptive purpose behind everything in life	Negativism/spiritual ignorance	Miserable are the negative who refuse to see or accept God's purposes

DISCIPLESHIP

Matthew 5:13–16 summarizes the importance of living according to kingdom righteousness.

To what does Jesus liken His disciples? (v. 13)

Why is it so important that we live out the kingdom life within ourselves? (v. 13)

If disciples become foolish and forget the importance of their influence on society, unredeemed humankind prevails virtually without contest. In effect, the kingdom of God loses its ability to influence, being "trampled underfoot by men."

What is Jesus' second metaphor? (v. 14)

What is the purpose of light? (v. 15)

What is Jesus' exhortation? (v. 16)

Disciples are to live so as to display the kingdom of God before men. When so doing, we manifest to others not only Jesus Christ but all the truth of the Law and the Prophets.

ON MURDER

Hagner explains how the next section of the Sermon is designed: "By means of six bold antitheses representing the teachings of Jesus, Matthew (5:21–48) now contrasts Jesus' exposition of the true and ultimate meaning of the Torah [the Law] with the more common, rabbinic understandings of the commandments. In this way the incomparable ethical demands of the kingdom are set forth, and in this way examples are provided showing how the righteousness of the Pharisees is to be exceeded."[4]

Jesus accomplishes this purpose through the formula, "You have heard" (referring to the common rabbinical understanding) "but I say to you" (reflecting His understanding). Jesus is not opposing the commandments themselves, but rather an inadequate or self-justifying understanding of them. His first concern is the sixth Commandment (Ex. 20:13). Read Matthew 5:21–26.

According to Exodus 21:12–14, what is "the judgment" to which Jesus refers? (v. 21)

What is the real problem behind murder? (v. 22)

"The sixth Commandment not only prohibits the actual deed of murder, but extends to thought and word, to unrighteous anger and destructive insults. 'Raca' is a colloquial expression of contempt for someone's mind, similar to 'blockhead,' or 'stupid,' while 'fool' expresses contempt for someone's character. They both insinuate the person should be doomed to hell. 'The council' initially designated the synagogue, but at the writing of this Gospel it may have referred to an investigative body of the church. 'Hell fire' is literally 'Gehenna,' the Greek translation of the Hebrew 'Valley of Hinnom.' The valley was a ravine south of Jerusalem where refuse was burned. It was most likely symbolic of the fires and judgments of Hades itself."[5]

Jesus is not suggesting a gradation or climax of punishments. He is speaking hyperbolically and urgently (vv. 25–26) to show the severity of godless inner attitudes, especially when they are sanctioned by one's religious system. The scribes and Pharisees taught that this Commandment meant you could hate your enemies in your heart, because there is no sin until you have killed someone.

So important is dealing with anger that it is even to take precedence over what? (vv. 23–24)

ON ADULTERY

Jesus' second antithesis deals with the seventh Commandment (Ex. 20:14). He again emphasizes one's thoughts, for to the Jews adulterous thoughts were not considered sinful. Read Matthew 5:27–32.

Where is the root of the sin of adultery? (v. 28)

How does this root attitude manifest itself? (v. 28)

What is Jesus' solution to this problem? (vv. 29–30)

Since the root of sin is the heart, maiming the body will not solve the problem. Jesus is again speaking hyperbolically to make a point, that discipleship often requires drastic practical steps to flee sin, accompanied by unreserved yielding to the Spirit for inner transformation.

ON DIVORCE

The four remaining antitheses deal with acts rather than thoughts. This passage on divorce, Matthew 5:31–32, needs to be interpreted with Matthew 19:3–12.

Read Matthew 5:31–32. Jesus' reference in verse 31 is to Deuteronomy 24:1–4. What seems to be the purpose behind Moses' instructions?

According to Jesus in Matthew 19:8, why did Moses give these divorce regulations? With what are these regulations in tension?

It is crucial to note that Jesus' answer is not intended to be a complete theology on divorce (we know this from 1 Corinthians 7). But what He said is pointed and clearly in response to a "test" from the Pharisees (v. 3). They want to trap Him into taking sides with one of their two conflicting rabbinical interpretations on divorce. There was "easy" divorce, "for just any reason," advocated by Rabbi Hillel. And there was "hard" divorce, "for sexual immorality" only, advocated by Rabbi Shammai. Neither addressed the heart issues behind divorce (see Gen. 2:24; Mal. 2:16).

What is Jesus' one specifically stated basis for biblically sanctioned divorce? (Matt. 5:32; see 1 Cor. 7:12–16 for another given by Paul.)

WORD WEALTH

Sexual immorality comes from the Greek word *porneia*, from which we get "pornography." *Porneia* describes sexual sins of any sort, prostitution, pedophilia, homosexuality, bestiality, lesbianism, incest, adultery, and so on. *Sexual immorality* may be part of the idea behind divorce for *some uncleanness* in Deuteronomy 24:1. Jesus does not indicate what number of such sexual encounters constitute a basis for divorce, nor does He state that the offended party *must* initiate divorce.

Divorces that are not biblically legal result in what? (Matt. 5:32)

Again, Jesus is painting with broad brush strokes in Matthew 5 and 19, which Paul fills in with some details (1 Cor. 7). Jesus' purpose in the Sermon was to teach that kingdom people need a driving passion for preserving marriage and a sober awareness of the consequences of a biblically illegal divorce.

ON OATHS

The Old Testament allowed for oath taking, or vows, as a means of affirming one's resolve to do something. By Jesus' day, however, oaths were being used selfishly to avoid commitment. No specific commandment is mentioned here. Jesus is addressing the Old Testament view about oaths and truthfulness (see Lev. 19:12; Num. 30:2; Deut. 23:21–23).

Read Matthew 5:33–37. What is Jesus' point? (v. 37; see James 5:12)

Any form of untruthfulness finds its origin in whom? (v. 37)

Old Testament oaths were binding because they were sworn in the LORD'S (Yahweh's) name. What were people apparently doing to skirt responsibility for carrying out oaths? (vv. 34–36)

ON RETALIATION

Jesus again contrasts two patterns of individual conduct to show the influence of the kingdom on one's ethics. His reference is to Exodus 21:24, Leviticus 24:20, and Deuteronomy 19:21, passages given not "to encourage personal revenge, but to protect the offender from punishment harsher than his offense warranted."[6]

Read Matthew 5:38–42. What is to be our attitude toward *demanding* personal rights? (v. 39)

Jesus is not advocating submission to abusive behavior, nor is He advocating evil to go uncontested. He is dealing with the matter of not *demanding* personal rights, especially at the expense of entrusting oneself "to Him who judges righteously" (1 Pet. 2:23). R. T. France supplies a helpful distinction: "A willingness to forgo one's personal rights, and to allow oneself to be insulted and imposed upon, is not incompatible with a firm stand for matters of principle and for the rights of others (see Paul's attitude in Acts 16:37; 22:25; 25:8–12). Indeed the principle of just retribution is not so much abrogated here as bypassed, in favor of an attitude which refuses to insist on one's rights, however legitimate. Jesus is . . . demanding an attitude which sits loose to personal rights."[7]

By way of illustrating these attitudes, Jesus gives two examples of responses to unreasonable requests. What is to be our attitude if we unjustifiably lose a legal battle, or if someone presses us to do something unreasonable? (v. 40, 41)

What is to be our attitude when someone wants something from us that may inconvenience us, especially financially? (v. 42)

ON LOVING ONE'S ENEMIES

Dealing with a tough Christian virtue, this final antithesis acts as a summation of the previous ones. It also brings Jesus to an important concern, "Therefore, you shall be perfect, just as your Father in heaven is perfect" (Matt. 5:48).

Read Matthew 5:43–48. What is Jesus' concern? (v. 43)

"You shall love your neighbor" is a quote from Leviticus 19:18. "Hate your enemy" represented a commonly held inference among the Jews, based on passages like Psalm 139:21–22 and Deuteronomy 7:2. But it was not taught in the Old Testament. One's "neighbor" referred to a fellow Jew; one's "enemy" referred to a Gentile. (This was not necessarily true of all in Jesus' day, but the self-justifying practice of many.)

What is Jesus' startling statement? (v. 44; see 5:10–12)

Loving behavior toward one's enemies is really what? (v. 45)

"The evil" here are God's enemies, those outside a personal relationship with Him through redemption in Christ Jesus.

How does Jesus illustrate His point? (vv. 46–47)

What is Jesus' conclusion? (v. 48)

WORD WEALTH

Perfect, *teleios*, comes "from *telos,* 'end.' *Teleios* refers to that which has reached an end, that is, finished, complete, perfect. When applied to persons, it signifies consummate soundness, and includes the idea of being whole. More particularly, when applied to believers, it denotes maturity."[8] The ethical standards of the kingdom cannot be satisfied short of this Godlike wholeness; though never reached in consummate form in this life, perfection represents the goal toward which Christ's disciples are to strive (see Eph. 4:1).

RELIGIOUS PRACTICES

The Sermon takes on a different emphasis in Matthew 6:1–18, as Jesus deals with three important charitable deeds: acts of mercy or kindness (vv. 2–4), prayer (vv. 5–15), and fasting (vv. 16–18). He is not criticizing these practices but examining motives (5:16). "Take heed that you do not do your charitable deeds before men, to be seen by them" (v. 1) governs His intent.

Read Matt. 6:1–4 and note the following.

What happens when someone practices charitable deeds *before men?* (v. 1)

Jesus is vague in the Sermon about what the Father's reward will be (5:12: 6:4, 6, 18). His intent is clear, however. Only that which is motivated to glorify God rather than self will be rewarded by God.

Citing religious fanfare, Jesus notes that doing charitable deeds before men is a self-glorifying _____ (v. 2).

BEHIND THE SCENES

> The Expositor's Bible Commentary notes that "the reference to trumpet announcements is difficult. [While] there is no evidence that the almsgivers themselves really blew trumpets on their way to the temple, the best answer seems to be that public fasts were proclaimed by the sounding of trumpets. At such times prayers for rain were recited in the streets (v. 5), and it was widely thought that alms-giving insured the efficacy of the fasts and prayers. These occasions afforded golden opportunities for ostentation."[9]

What is to be the Christian's *heart attitude* when doing acts of mercy or kindness? (vv. 3–4)

THE DISCIPLE AND WEALTH

Jesus now moves to a disciple's dependence on God (Matt. 6:19–34). His instruction, Hagner notes, is designed to "contrast the pursuit of the wealth of this world with the single-hearted desire of the disciple to do the will of the Father, wherein alone lies true wealth."[10]

Read Matthew 6:19–24 and note the following. Committed discipleship requires what? (vv. 19–20; Luke 12:16–21)

Where we invest our greatest energies is an expression of what? (v. 21)

If one's eye is good, e.g., if a disciple's focus is Godward and not wealthward, what will that Christian's life be like? (v. 22)

If one's eye is bad, e.g., focus is wealthward rather than Godward, what will that Christian's life be like? (v. 23)

Selfish materialism can never direct us toward meaningful discipleship.

Jesus concludes by stating that partially committed, or part-time, discipleship is impossible (v. 24; Matt. 10:34–39; 16:24–26). Why?

 WORD WEALTH

Mammon comes from the Greek *mamonas,* which is a transliteration of the Aramaic noun *mamon,* meaning wealth or property. It may be derived from a Hebrew word for "treasure" (Gen. 43:23), and it is clearly able to control one's will (Matt. 6:24).

THE DISCIPLE AND ANXIETY

If the disciple is not to be preoccupied with material gain, how will basic needs be met? This is Jesus' concern in Matthew 6:24–34, especially as it relates to kingdom priorities (v. 33). It is built around the exhortation not to *worry.*

 WORD WEALTH

Worry, *merimnao,* comes "from *merizo,* 'to divide into parts.' The word suggests a distraction, a preoccupation with things causing anxiety, stress, and pressure."[11] It has overtones of fearful anxiety, often causing sleeplessness.

Read Matthew 6:25–34 and note the following. Why should disciples not worry about basic subsistence? (v. 25)

What must be realized to prevent inordinate anxiety about physical needs? (vv. 26, 32)

What is the disciple's top priority? What results from adopting that priority? (v. 33)

God has not only the present under control but the _____ as well (v. 34).

"Sufficient for the day *is* its own trouble," is a proverbial saying about the absurdity of being anxious about the future when we live in today. Hagner comments: "The disciples have a 'heavenly Father' who knows of their ongoing needs and who will supply them. The passage does not mean, however, that food, drink, clothing, and other such necessities will come to the disciples automatically without work or foresight. It addresses only the problem of anxiety about these things."[12]

FAITH ALIVE

Are you sensitive to the fact that your pursuits reflect your heart's desires? Do you have affections that are misplaced? Do you have fear or anxiety about daily life? Are you perhaps struggling with believing that God will care for you? Do you seek security in possessions more than in God? Honestly and openly before God's Word, assess yourself in light of these questions and our exploration of Matthew 6:19–34.

DO NOT JUDGE

Jesus' concern in Matthew 7:1–5 is that His disciples see no place in kingdom ethics for a condemning, judgmental attitude toward others in the household of faith. Many scholars see it as an expansion of the fifth petition in the Lord's Prayer, "And forgive us our debts, as we forgive our debtors" (Matt. 6:12).

Read Matthew 7:1–5. What is Jesus' prohibition? (v. 1)

This is not a prohibition against being discerning; nor is Jesus saying never to pass judgment against people (see Matt. 7:6; 18:15–18; 1 Cor. 5:4–5). "Judge" (Greek, *krino*) in context means "condemn" (see Rom. 14:10–13). Jesus is prohibiting censorious, unfair judgments which desire punishment rather than corrective discipline.

What will happen if one assumes this judgmental attitude? (v. 1–2; see Rom. 2:1)

"Will be judged" means that God is the One who will so judge.

Why are self-righteous, censorious critics unhelpful among Christ's disciples? (vv. 3–5)

"Speck" refers to anything small (perhaps sawdust) that gets in one's eye. It is a metaphor for slight or insignificant shortcomings in one's life. "A plank" (log) is an extreme exaggeration for contrast.

What enables a disciple to speak to (judge) the shortcomings in other disciples? (v. 5; see 1 Cor. 11:31; Gal. 6:1)

Lest His disciples lose all discernment and their sense of "healthy judging," Jesus reminds them of what they are to do when they encounter resistance or hostility toward the gospel. What is the command? (v. 6; see Matt. 10:13–14)

"What is holy" and "pearls" are references to the gospel of the kingdom (see Matt. 13:45–46). "Dogs" and "swine" refer to anyone who is willfully and repeatedly unreceptive.

THE GOLDEN RULE

This one verse, the famous "Golden Rule," is known in just about every culture. It is an expansion of Leviticus 19:18 (see Matt. 22:34–40). Its importance to Christianity is summarized by Paul when he writes, "but the greatest of these [virtues] is love" (1 Cor. 13:13).

Read Matthew 7:12. What is the scope of our deeds of love?

When a disciple does good deeds, what is reflected? (Matt. 7:11)

As Jesus' disciples obey this commandment, what are they fulfilling? (See comments on Matt. 5:17 above.)

TWO WAYS

The ethical teachings of the Sermon are now complete. Jesus concludes with a series of warnings, all of which are built on strong contrasts, and which climax with a parable. He begins by inviting His disciples to travel along the way He has been outlining.

Read Matthew 7:13–14 and note the following.

To what two things does Jesus liken the rigors of committed discipleship? (v. 14)

Are committed disciples the majority or minority? (v. 14)

Though discipleship is rigorous, why is it worth the rigors? (v. 14)

THE GENUINE AND THE FALSE

Kingdom disciples must be able to recognize that which is from God and that which is not, be it ethical standards, teachings, or persons. In this penultimate section of the Sermon, Jesus speaks about recognizing false prophets (vv. 15–20) and false commitment (vv. 21–23).

Read Matthew 7:15–23. False prophets look like the people of God, but what are they? (v. 15)

How can we detect them? (vv. 16–18, 20)

It is contrary to the laws of nature for a good tree (representative of truly committed disciples of the kingdom) to bear bad fruit (see James 3:12). Hence, it is the unrighteous conduct of the false prophets that betrays their character. In the Sermon, righteousness is indicated by what disciples do, not only by what they say.

What is their final fate if they do not repent? (v. 19)

Jesus illustrates what He has taught by referring to people making impressive claims. What are their claims? (v. 22)

What is Jesus' response to their claims? (v. 23)

Though claiming impressive ministry, they have something fundamental missing in their lives. What is it? (v. 21)

These persons are not criticized for their activities per se, and it is beyond the intent of the Sermon to ask, "Are they truly 'born-again' people? If not, how could they do these things?" Jesus' intent is to teach religious activities are no substitute for righteousness. Again, it is not so much what we *say* ("Lord, Lord") but how we *live* that matters.

THE PARABLE OF TWO BUILDERS

Jesus concludes with a powerful parable about obedience and how it will help disciples survive the pressures of life today. It is not a teaching about "salvation by works," but a sober reminder that salvation by grace through faith is not cheap. Imputed righteousness and subsequent conduct are more closely linked in God's mind than we may think. When the kingdom is present, a call to its ethical demands is reasonable. Read Matthew 7:24–29 and note the following.

In light of the Sermon, what makes a man wise? (v. 24; see James 1:22–25)

Why does this person survive? (v. 25)

What is the multitude's overall response to the Sermon and why? (vv. 28–29)

Jesus has authority in Himself. He does not teach merely by repeating the traditions of other teachers. His authority overwhelms the hearers. "The people" (v. 29) refers to the Sermon's secondary audience who apparently join Jesus and His disciples during the teaching (see Matt. 5:1).

1. George Ladd, *A Theology of the New Testament* (Grand Rapids: Eerdmans, 1974), 128.
2. *Spirit-Filled Life Bible*, 1411, note on Matt. 5:17.
3. Donald A. Hagner, *Word Biblical Commentary: Matthew* (Dallas: Word, 1993), 91.
4. Ibid., 111.
5. *Spirit-Filled Life Bible*, 1411–1412, note on Matt. 5:22.
6. *Spirit-Filled Life Bible*, 1413, note on Matt. 5:38–42.
7. *Spirit-Filled Life Bible*, 1898, "Word Wealth: James 3:2 perfect."
8. Frank E. Gaebelein, ed., *The Expositor's Bible Commentary*, Vol. 8 (Grand Rapids: Zondervan, 1984), 164.
9. Hagner, *Matthew*, 156.
10. *Spirit-Filled Life Bible*, 1415, "Word Wealth: Matt. 6:25 worry."
11. Hagner, *Matthew*, 166–67.

Lesson 8/On Fasting and Prayer

Fasting and prayer, especially fasting, evoke all kinds of responses, and a lot of them are negative ones. To Jesus, however, these two disciplines are simply regular matter-of-fact aspects of Christian discipleship. Indeed, they are privileges which can release great blessing.

And as we will see, fasting is another spiritual discipline that releases great blessing. Furthermore, Jesus, in the Sermon on the Mount, placed fasting in as normal and regular a practice as giving and praying. Unfortunately, we're often far from that. But fasting is necessary at times to move the supernatural world and give us closer communion with God.

Let's keep these things in mind as we look at what the synoptic Gospels teach about fasting and prayer.

JESUS' PRAYER LIFE

Much of our understanding about prayer in the Synoptics comes from what Jesus models. Luke particularly is interested in Jesus' prayer life, clearly intimating in 22:39 that prayer was one of Jesus' customs, along with Sabbath day worship (Luke 4:16).

According to Luke 3:21, what attends "the heavens [being] opened" to Jesus at His baptism?

According to Luke 5:15–16, how does Jesus handle the temptation to become a popular miracle worker and the stress of pressing duties?

According to Luke 6:12–13, what does Jesus do before choosing key men to be future leaders of His work?

According to Luke 9:18–20, what does Jesus do prior to asking His disciples to give their perspective about His identity?

According to Luke 9:28–29, what is Jesus doing when He is transfigured?

According to Luke 11:1, what effect does Jesus' prayer life have on His disciples?

According to Luke 22:39–46, how does Jesus deal with the overwhelming realization of His impending death?

According to Luke 23:46, Jesus dies doing what?

Jesus prayed before decisions and crises. What can be surmised from this?

Luke also tells us that Jesus prayed for Peter (22:31) and for His enemies (23:34). On at least four occasions, Luke notes that Jesus exhorted His disciples to pray. Read the following passages and note what they are told to pray for.

Luke 6:28

Luke 11:2

Luke 22:40, 46

The temptation (Luke 22:40) which Jesus mentions probably refers to what He had just said (Luke 22:28–38). Prayer will enable them to remain firm amidst the trials awaiting them.

In Matthew 6:5, Jesus warns against what type of prayer? (see Mark 12:38–40)

What should be our motive when we pray? (Matt. 6:6)

 WORD WEALTH

Pray, *proseuchomai.* "The word is progressive. Starting with the noun, *euche,* which is a prayer to God that also includes making a vow, the word expands to the verb *euchomai,* a special term describing an invocation, request, or entreaty. Adding *pros,* 'in the direction of' (God), *proseuchomai* becomes the most frequent word for prayer."[1]

Not only does Jesus model prayer and call His disciples to practice it; He gives instruction as well, as is seen in two of His more well-known parables, "The Friend at Midnight" (Luke 11:5–13) and "The Widow and the Judge" (Luke 18:1–8), and in the Lord's Prayer (Matt. 6:7–15).

THE FRIEND AT MIDNIGHT

Read Luke 11:5–13 and note the following. What is the situation of the arriving friend and why doesn't the person inside want to answer the request? (vv. 5–7)

Why does the man within finally answer the request? (v. 8)

WORD WEALTH

Persistence, *anaideia,* literally means "shamelessness, importunity, or over-boldness." It describes a type of brassiness. "It isn't the brassiness of a smart aleck making demands, but the forwardness of a person who is so taken with an awareness of need that he abandons normal protocol. Jesus is saying, 'Your first barrier isn't God, it's your own hesitance to ask freely. You need to learn the kind of boldness that isn't afraid to ask—whatever the need or the circumstance.' "[2]

Jesus follows this somewhat humorous parable about importunity with direct instruction on what is involved (vv. 9–10), as well as a reminder of the willing nature of the Father we are addressing (vv. 11–13).

What is Jesus' instruction? (v. 9)

What must we understand in order to ask, seek, and knock effectively? (v. 10)

WORD WEALTH

Aitein [to ask] refers to the act of praying where the will is earnestly fixed on the answering of the prayer. So the desire is not merely a vague or halfhearted one. *Zetein* means "to seek with the object of finding or obtaining." So this includes faithful prayer and all other exertion directed towards the purpose of obtaining the things for which the prayer is offered. While confidently awaiting God's answer, the one who prays must also from his side do everything that is necessary. *Krouein,* "to knock," refers to the urgent sincerity exercised in praying and seeking. All three verbs refer to the continuous, uninterrupted act.[3]

What more can be learned about "asking" from Matthew 18:18–20; 20:21–22, John 14:12–14, and Ephesians 3:20–21? What more can be learned about "seeking" from Matthew 6:33, John 5:30, and Colossians 3:1?

What do we learn in Luke 11:11–13 (see Matt. 7:9–11) about the Fatherhood of God to help us pray?

THE WIDOW AND THE JUDGE

Read Luke 18:1–8 and note the following. What is Jesus' purpose in teaching this parable? (v. 1)

What is the nature of the judge? (vv. 2, 4) What is the widow doing? (vv. 3, 5)

Why does the judge avenge her? (v. 5)

WORD WEALTH

Weary, *hupopiadzo,* literally means "to strike under the eye; to give a black eye to." The idea is that in her continued coming to the judge she will somehow socially defame him for refusing to grant her request. It is really a selfishly motivated response of the judge's, not one of compassion.

How does Jesus apply the parable to our prayer life? (vv. 6–8)

THE LORD'S PRAYER

Pastor Jack Hayford says, "It's the most prayed prayer in the world: the Lord's Prayer, we call it. Some challenge that designation, saying, 'It's the disciples' prayer—He gave it to them, told them to pray it.' But He is the one who taught it. He is the one who breathed its depth of insight."[4]

The prayer (with slight variations) is recorded in Matthew 6 and Luke 11. In Matthew, it is part of the Sermon on the Mount dealing with a disciple's motives in religious responsibilities (6:1–18; see "Religious Practices" in chapter 7). In

Luke (11:1–4), it is presented in answer to the request, "Lord, teach us to pray" (v. 1).

In Luke, Jesus introduces the prayer by saying, "When you pray, say . . ." (v. 2). In Matthew, He introduces it by saying, "In this manner . . . pray . . ." (v. 9). This implies that Jesus intended it to be prayed both literally (Luke) and in principle (Matthew).

Read Matthew 6:7–15 and note the following. Because God will not be manipulated through repeated, maybe even magical, phrases, what is Jesus' warning? (v. 7; see Mark 12:38–40)

⚔ WORD WEALTH

Vain repetitions, *battalogeo,* has the idea of babbling by repeating meaningless syllables uttered mechanically without thought. The heathen rather than the hypocrites (vv. 5, 16) are referred to because, as R. T. France notes, "prayer in the non-Jewish world was often characterized particularly by formal invocation and magical incantations, in which the correct repetition counted rather than the worshipper's attitude or intention."[5]

Why does the disciple not have to pray empty phrases? (v. 8)

For prayer to be effective, what must we understand about God? (v. 9)

New Testament prayer is based on understanding the nature of the Father and our relationship to Him. "Father" (Greek, *pater*) is equivalent to the Aramaic word, *'abba,* an affectionate and intimate term children used to address their earthly fathers. It emphasizes our intimate relationship with God. "In heaven" emphasizes His transcendence. "As Father, God is concerned for the needs of His children; as the One in heaven, He is all-powerful."[6]

The prayer proper (vv. 9–13) consists of seven petitions, each one establishing a principle around which effective prayer is built. The first three petitions are "You" petitions addressed to God. They concern His glory and purposes. The final four are "We" petitions, emphasizing the disciples' present needs. Read these verses and note the petition and the principles they establish.

Petition #1 (v. 9)

"Hallowed be" (Greek, *hagiadzo*) is a petition for God to reveal Himself and His purposes ("Your name") in history, especially among those before whom it has been profaned (see Ezek. 36:23). Inherent in the petition is an expression of committed worship, the petitioner making himself available to the Father through righteous living and availability to His service.

Petition #2 (v. 10)

The kingdom as taught and demonstrated by Jesus brings God's sovereign rulership in Jesus into our lives and situations now. It is also a petition that it ultimately come in consummation. This specifies how God will hallow His name.

Petition #3 (v. 10)

This is somewhat synonymous with petition #2, which is perhaps why it is missing in Luke's account (Luke 11:2). Its distinction from the previous petition lies in its implied request of the petitioner to live the kingdom ethics necessary to advance kingdom purposes. Hagner notes that "there is a sense in which the first three petitions of the prayer are also a prayer that the disciples will be faithful to their calling, that they will do their part (in obedience), not to bring the kingdom but to manifest its prophetic presence through Jesus and the Spirit."[7]

Petition #4 (v. 11)

The significance of this petition is contested among scholars, primarily because the Greek word translated "daily" (*epi-*

ousion) is obscure. Most are in agreement, however, that it is a petition for God to supply the day-to-day necessities of life, with the realization that the provision is itself a blessing from heaven. Pastor Hayford comments that "the most important thing about this is not the discovery that we can ask for God's help in the mundane matters of our personal lives. The most important thing is that we are told to [ask]. . . . Back-to-back with prayer that the Almighty's will be worked on earth, we should not overlook the simplest matters of life."[8]

Petition #5 (v. 12)

"Debts" (Greek, *opheilemata*) is from the Aramaic concept of sin as a debt owed to God. It refers to our failures and shortcomings before Him (see Luke's "sins" [11:4]). Jesus explains the matter of forgiving our debtors in verses 14–15.

Petition #6 (v. 13)

This is also a difficult petition because of the ambiguity of a Greek word, *peirasmos,* translated here as "temptation." Should it be rendered "temptation" or "testing"? Both are legitimate renderings of the Greek, yet both have their own difficulties because of other scriptures (1 Cor. 10:13; James 1:2–3, 13). We will reserve judgment until we look at the final petition.

Petition #7 (v. 13)

The conjunction "but," here, presupposes we will face the difficulties defined as *peirasmos* in petition #6, and that "the evil one" will want to take advantage of those difficulties to bring destructive ends. Thus, as to the meaning of *peirasmos* in petition #6, note the following explanation by Hayford: "What we have here [v. 13] is a special facet of prayer which Jesus taught; one which cannot be understood apart from linking it with the last part of the sentence [v. 13]. The two work in tandem: 'Don't bring us in, but bring us out!'"[9]

"The spirit of the text argues that we understand the Lord's instruction as a summons to maturity. He is saying, 'When you pray, acknowledge that the Father isn't your problem when temptation assails you, but that He is your protector.'"

Assuming the traditional ending of the prayer is to be retained (most scholars agree the textual evidence in its favor is weak [see Luke 11:4]), how does the prayer close? (v. 13)

Matthew 6:14–15 (see Mark 11:25) is not part of the prayer. It is an elaboration of the fifth petition (v. 12), stating that principle positively (v. 14) and negatively (v. 15). What is the point? (see Matt. 18:23–35)

FAITH AND PRAYER

James is quite clear about faith and prayer. "Let him ask in faith, with no doubting, for he who doubts is like a wave of the sea driven and tossed by the wind. For let not that man suppose that he will receive anything from the Lord" (1:6–7). Jesus' teachings on prayer in the Synoptics reflect this same truth. "And whatever things you ask in prayer, believing, you will receive" (Matt. 21:22). Let's examine a couple of passages on the role of faith in prayer.

 WORD WEALTH

Faith, *pistis,* means "conviction, confidence, trust, belief, reliance, trustworthiness, and persuasion. In the New Testament setting, *pistis* is the divinely implanted principle of inward confidence, assurance, trust, and reliance in God and all that He says."[10] With specific reference to prayer, faith is a relationship of practical trust with the One to whom you are praying. This trust stems from understanding both the nature and will of God.

HAVE FAITH IN GOD

In Mark 11:12–14, Jesus curses a fig tree and it withers. "The fig tree is used here to designate Israel of Jesus' time, whose religious system and heritage appeared to hold promise of satisfaction. So the curse extended not only to the tree but also to the nation of Israel, an enacted parable, showing the judgment that was to come upon Israel's false profession."[11] Jesus does not interpret the significance of the event itself; instead, He uses it to teach a lesson on releasing heaven's resources into life's situations. Read Mark 11:20–24.

What prompts Jesus' teaching on faith and prayer? (v. 21)

What is Jesus' immediate response? (v. 22)

How does Jesus illustrate the point He has just made? (v. 23)

"Mountain" here symbolizes any type of great difficulty or hindrance (see Zech. 4:7).

What is Jesus' conclusion? (v. 24)

God is always ready to respond to resolute faith that demonstrates itself in prayer (see Is. 65:24). The following quote summarizes the importance of Jesus' teaching here: "From Jesus' own lips we receive the most direct and practical instruction concerning our exercise of faith. Consider three points: (1) It is to be 'in God.' Faith that speaks is first faith that seeks. The Almighty One is the Source and Grounds of our faith and being. Faith only flows *to* Him because of the faithfulness that flows *from* Him. (2) Faith is not a trick performed with our lips, but a spoken expression that springs from the conviction of our hearts. The idea that faith's confession is a 'formula' for getting things from God is unbiblical. But the fact that the faith in our hearts is to be spoken, and thereby become active and effective toward specific results, is taught here by the Lord Jesus. (3) Jesus' words 'whatever things' apply this principle to every aspect of our lives. The only restrictions are (a) that our faith be 'in God' our living Father and in alignment with His will and word; and (b) that we 'believe'—not doubting in our hearts. Thus, 'speaking to the mountain' is not a vain or superstitious exercise or indulgence in humanistic mind-science, but instead becomes an applied release of God's creative word of promise."[12]

PRAYER AND THE DEMONIC

Of the many "mountains" encountered in prayer, confrontation with the demonic is perhaps the most poignant. Demons, or unclean spirits, move in Satan's authority. Hence, encounters with them are in fact encounters with Satan and his power. (See "Releasing the Demonized" in chapter 4.) From one such encounter, Matthew 17:14–21, we learn how to pray when dealing with the demonic and what hinders effective prayer. Read this passage and note the following.

Describe the situation. (vv. 14–15)

Why is this man asking Jesus' help? (v. 16)

What is Jesus' initial response? (v. 17)

Jesus' response indicates that the disciples' failure here is to some degree symbolic of the entire nation of Israel in her failure to respond to His messianic mission (see Matt. 12:38–45; Deut. 32:5, 20).

How does Jesus deal with the demon? (v. 18)

WORD WEALTH

Rebuked, *epitimao,* can also be translated "subdued." According to Robert Guelich, *epitimao* "has a technical meaning coming from the underlying Hebrew word *ga'ar,* meaning a commanding word 'uttered by God or by his spokesman, by which evil powers are brought into submission.' "[13]

When the demonic is involved, a disciple's "prayer" is to be that of speaking directly to the unclean spirit to cease activity and depart. This is possible because disciples are delegated agents of God's kingdom.

Though representative on one hand of the larger picture (v. 17), the disciples have a unique problem that prevents the exorcism. What is it? (v. 20)

A distinction needs to be made between Jesus' accusation in Matthew 17:17 and Matthew 17:20. In verse 17, the problem is a failing to accept the kingdom reign of God through Jesus, His Messiah (see Mark 6:6). In verse 20, the problem is the disciples' little or underdeveloped faith. It does not mean outright unbelief or distrust, but faith that is not sufficiently developed to deal with the situation at hand (see Matt. 6:30; 8:26; 14:31; 16:8). We might term it "immature faith," requiring more understanding and experience to mature.

BINDING AND LOOSING

Throughout our study we have emphasized certain responsibilities and privileges of Christ's disciples. Another such authoritative privilege is that which Jesus terms binding and loosing on earth (Matt. 16:19). This authority is exercised to a large extent through prayer. Jesus teaches this principle in conjunction with a key confession of His messiahship. Read Matthew 16:13–20 and note the following.

Who makes the significant confession? (v. 16)

What is Jesus' response to the confession? (v. 17)

What does Jesus say He will build upon this confession? (v. 18)

What does He promise His church? (v. 18)

"The expression *gates of Hades* means 'the power of death' cannot prevent the advance of the kingdom, nor claim victory over those who belong to God."[14]

What is given to His church as a weapon against the power of death? (v. 19)

"I will give you the keys of the kingdom of heaven" is like saying, "I will hand over to you delegated authority or control to minister kingdom power as I would."

How is this delegated authority to be exercised? (v. 19)

What application does verse 19 have to individual believers as they face life's daily problems?

"The implications of this significant verse are diverse and need to be understood. *Keys* denote authority. Jesus is passing on to His church His authority or control to *bind* and to *loose on earth. Will be bound* and *will be loosed* indicate that Jesus is the One who has activated the provisions through His Cross; the church is then charged with implementation of what He has released through His life, death, and resurrection.

"Clearly rabbinic in imagery, binding and loosing have to do with forbidding or permitting. In other words, Jesus is stating that the church will be empowered to continue in the privileged responsibility of leavening the earth with His kingdom power and provision. For example, if someone is bound by sin, the church can 'loose' him by preaching the provision of freedom from sin in Jesus Christ (Rom. 6:14). If someone is indwelt by a demon, the church can 'bind' the demon by commanding its departure (Acts 16:18), realizing that Jesus alone made this provision possible (Matt. 12:29). How the church binds and looses is diverse and would most certainly extend far beyond the mere use of these terms in prayerful petitions."[15]

Matthew 18:15–20 may be an application of this authority in matters of church discipline.

ON FASTING

Fasting is "going without food or drink voluntarily, generally for religious purposes. Fasting, however, could also be done for other reasons. It was sometimes done as a sign of distress, grief, or repentance."[16] Prayer is to accompany fasting. In the Synoptics, we find Anna (Luke 2:37), John the Baptist and his disciples (Mark 2:18), the Pharisees (Matt. 9:14), and Jesus (Matt. 4:2) fasting. For Jesus, it is a given that His disciples will practice this discipline (Matt. 6:16); however, as with other spiritual disciplines, He must give careful instruction.

MOTIVE AND FASTING

Jesus' final teaching in His triad on proper kingdom motives for religious disciplines (Matt. 6:1–18) deals with fasting (vv. 16–18). As with acts of mercy or kindness and prayer, so with fasting: the disciple's motive is of paramount importance.

Read Matthew 6:16–18 and note the following. What is Jesus' prohibition to His disciples? (v. 16)

What is the hypocrites' motive in disfiguring their faces? (v. 16)

"Disfigure" (Greek, *aphavidzo*) likely refers to making the face dirty with ashes. This was accompanied by a generally disheveled appearance to attract attention to a personal fast.

What is Jesus' command to His disciples? (v. 17) Why does He so command? (v. 18)

Hagner notes that "In view here is a special instance of grooming (see 2 Sam. 12:20; Eccl. 9:8) and personal enjoyment, a sign of happiness that was forbidden on fast days. Jesus thus exhorts even an extra measure of care to one's appearance, so that it could not give the slightest hint that one was fasting."[17]

WHEN TO FAST

During Jesus' time with His disciples, they did not fast regularly, and this concerned John the Baptist's disciples who fasted often. Read Matthew 9:14–17 and note why Jesus did not have His disciples fasting during His earthly ministry.

What reason does Jesus give for not having His disciples practice fasting? (v. 15)

Will this always be the case for His followers? (v. 15; see Acts 13:2–3; 14:23; and 1 Cor. 7:5 for the practice of fasting in the early church.)

What reason does Jesus give for this change from standard Jewish practice? (vv. 16–17)

 PROBING THE DEPTHS

Reasonable Jewish piety called for fasting on the Day of Atonement (see Lev. 16:29–31) and on the anniversaries of the many destructions of Jerusalem. The Pharisees of Jesus' day went far beyond this general practice with twice-a-week personal fasts. Their fasts were primarily designed to "try to get God" to bring about the messianic promises. Because His kingdom had already come (at least in part), Jesus radically changed the focus of fasting.

As Hagner explains, "All conduct is to be judged on the basis of [Jesus] and his teaching. There is accordingly something fundamentally incompatible between fasting and the joy of the kingdom. If fasting is conceived of as a lamenting or grieving over God's failure to act, if it is thought of as a way to hasten the coming of the Messiah, if it is thought of as a way of gaining God's favor, it is contradictory to what the gospel signifies. The Christian is not a person characterized by sorrow, sackcloth, and ashes, laments and fasting, but a person of joy who has experienced grace and fulfillment. There is a place for . . . fasting, but it [is] very different in nature from that practiced by the disciples of John and the Pharisees. It must be fasting within the larger framework of the fulfillment and joy of the kingdom already present in the Church. Fasting in this case will be a spiritual discipline practiced with prayer, for such purposes as sharpening one's focus or deepening one's experience."[18]

Although some scholars disagree (1) whether Matthew 17:21 was part of the original Greek manuscript or was added later by the church, and (2) whether "and fasting" should be added to the end of Mark 9:29, there is strong textual evidence that both are legitimate (especially the Mark ending). What does Jesus teach in these verses about the role of fasting in dealing with certain demonic activity?

 FAITH ALIVE

What has impacted you the most in this chapter?

Are there two or three areas in which you've gained new understanding or been reminded of something you've forgotten? If so, what changes do you see yourself making to practice these truths?

Realizing that understanding and practicing prayer usually cycles from discipline to duty to delight, where would you say you are on the continuum?

If fasting is not a regular discipline, could it be because you have not yet experienced the profound release and victory that this New Testament discipline brings in the lives of those who practice it?

1. *Spirit-Filled Life Bible*, 1414, "Word Wealth: Matthew 6:6 pray."
2. Jack Hayford, *Prayer Is Invading The Impossible* (New York: Ballantine, 1983), 49.
3. Norval Geldenhuys, *The New International Commentary on the New Testament: Luke* (Grand Rapids: Eerdmans, 1979), 326. Used by permission.
4. Hayford, *Prayer*, 90.
5. R. T. France, *Tyndale New Testament Commentaries: Matthew* (Grand Rapids: Eerdmans, 1986), 132.
6. Donald A. Hagner, *Word Biblical Commentary: Matthew* (Dallas: Word, 1993), 148.
7. Ibid., 149.
8. Hayford, *Prayer*, 95.
9. Ibid., 122.
10. *Spirit-Filled Life Bible*, 1492, "Word Wealth: Mark 11:22 faith."
11. Ibid., 1446, note on Matt. 21:19.
12. *Spirit-Filled Life Bible*, 1492, "Kingdom Dynamics: Mark 11:22–24, Jesus on 'Faith's Confession.' "
13. Robert Guelich, *Word Biblical Commentary: Mark* (Dallas: Word, 1989), 57.
14. *Spirit-Filled Life Bible*, note on Matt. 16:18.
15. Ibid., 1436, note on Matt. 16:19.
16. *Nelson's Illustrated Bible Dictionary*, 378.
17. Hagner, *Matthew*, 154.
18. Ibid., 244–245.

Lesson 9/Sunday to Thursday of the Final Week

Immediately following the Transfiguration, in which three privileged disciples glimpse Jesus' future glory and hear Him insist on suffering as the way to glory, Jesus begins the countdown to His crucifixion.[1] "Now it came to pass, when the time had come for Him to be received up, that He steadfastly set His face to go to Jerusalem" (Luke 9:51). It will take about one year to finally arrive, as He completes His later Judean ministry.

His arrival in Jerusalem approximately a year after the Transfiguration marked the beginning of His final week. In reading the Synoptics, we can sometimes forget the many events that occurred the last week: the Triumphal Entry, Jesus' weeping over Jerusalem, the temple cleansing, the cursing of the fig tree, questioning by the religious authorities, Jesus' woes to the Scribes and Pharisees, the Olivet Discourse, the Last Supper, and the entire series of Passion/Resurrection events. Jesus' teachings this week included the widow's mite, the Great Commandment, paying tribute to Caesar, and the parable of the wicked husbandman. It was a busy, history-changing week to say the least!

In the remaining chapters, we will examine crucial events and teachings of this week which have not already been discussed.

AT A GLANCE

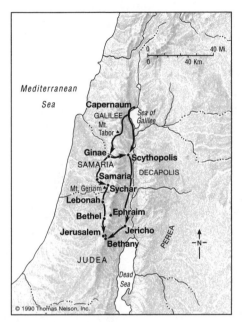

Jewish Pilgrimage from Galilee to Jerusalem. The popular route passed directly through Samaria. However, some pious Jews took an alternate route through Jericho to avoid Samaria.[2]

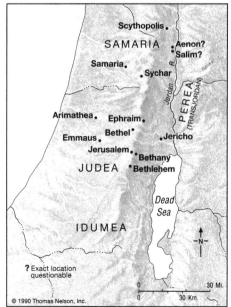

Last Journey to Jerusalem. Jesus' last ascent to Jerusalem began on the eastern side of the Jordan. After crossing the river, He entered Jericho, then ascended the mountain to Bethany and Jerusalem. There He was crucified.[3]

THE TRIUMPHAL ENTRY

We have here perhaps the most famous two-mile "demonstration" in human history. It is the Sunday before Good Friday, and it begins at Bethphage on the eastern slopes of the Mount of Olives. Shortly after the raising of Lazarus (John 11:1–44), public enthusiasm is apparently renewed to see this famous "Rabbi from Nazareth," whose admiration had somewhat waned because He refused to accommodate selfish demands (John 6:66). Furthermore, He had been spending time aside teaching His closest disciples since He knew the time was becoming short.

"What do you think—that He will not come to the feast?" (John 11:56) is the buzzword around Jerusalem during this Passover season, even as the chief priests and scribes accelerate their conspiracy against Jesus (Mark 11:18–19). The Triumphal Entry is recorded in all four Gospels. We will study Matthew's account.

Read Matthew 21:1–11 and note the following. Who initiates this event? (v. 1)

"The ride on a colt, because it was planned, could only be an acted parable, a deliberate act of symbolic self-disclosure for those with eyes to see or, after the Resurrection, with memories by which to remember and integrate the events of the preceding weeks and years. Secrecy was being lifted."[4]

What are the instructions? (vv. 2–3)

Matthew alone mentions two animals, and Mark notes that they are to find a "colt . . . on which no one has sat" (11:2).

What is the purpose behind this event? (vv. 4–5)

"Tell the daughter of Zion" (v. 5) is quoted from Isaiah 62:11; the rest of verse 5 is a quote from Zechariah 9:9. The donkey stands in contrast to the war horse of a military ruler, emphasizing that Jesus is not now coming as a military Messiah but as One who must first suffer.

What is the crowd's reaction? (vv. 8–9)

"A king's subject paid homage to him by providing a carpet for him to walk or ride on. *Hosanna* means 'Save now.' It was more than a cry of acclamation. Essentially, it was a plea from an oppressed people to their Savior for deliverance. Later it came to be a standard shout of praise. Psalm 118:25, 26, from which the quote comes, is messianic; therefore, the people were publicly acknowledging Jesus as the Messiah."[5]

What is the multitude's overall reaction upon His arrival in Jerusalem? (vv. 10–11) What about that of the religious leaders? (Matt. 21:14–16)

In the midst of the crowd's joy, Luke records a glaring contrast from Jesus Himself. Read Luke 19:41–44. What is Jesus' contrasting reaction and what prompts it? (v. 41)

Spiritually, where are the people of Jerusalem as a whole? (v. 42)

"They are hidden from your eyes" indicates satanic blindness (see Luke 9:43–45).

What will be the result? (vv. 43–44; see Is. 29:3; Ezek. 4:1–3)

THE SECOND TEMPLE CLEANSING

On Monday of the final week, Jesus returns from Bethany and goes immediately to the temple. He had stopped there on the previous day, but had only "looked around at all things, as the hour was already late" (Mark 11:11). The sorrow He had felt about Jerusalem the day before now turns to wrath, as He deals with a gross violation against the LORD God (see John

2:17). This is likely the second such action in the temple (see John 2:13–17).

Read Mark 11:15–19. What does Jesus do? (vv. 15–16)

Why does He do this? (v. 17)

"My house . . . all nations" is quoted from the Greek translation of Isaiah 56:7; "den of thieves" is an allusion to Jeremiah 7:11. William Lane points out that the Greek behind this second phrase stresses that the actions of the priestly authorities are beyond correction and leading toward the judgment of Mark 13:2. "The merchants are [like] marauders . . . because they were insensitive to the holiness of the area where they practiced their trade."[6]

How do the scribes and chief priests respond? (v. 18) The people? (v. 18)

THREE FORCEFUL PARABLES

Tuesday of the final week finds Jesus once again giving instruction in the temple (Mark 11:27). As the confrontation between Jesus and the Jewish religious leaders nears its climax, Jesus speaks three parables against them, all clarifying who is truly acceptable to God and on what basis. They follow the symbolic cursing of the fig tree (see "Have Faith in God" in chapter 8).

THE PARABLE OF THE TWO SONS

Read Matthew 21:28–32 and note the following. Who are the main characters in the parable? (vv. 28–30)

What is Jesus' personal application of the parable? (v. 31)

How do tax collectors and harlots gain entrance into the kingdom of God? (v. 32; see vv. 23–27)

The first son symbolizes the repentant who accept the requirements of the kingdom and endeavor to live them. The second son symbolizes the unrepentant religious leaders of Israel who only talk obedience. The religious leaders do not recognize the right way to God, even though they saw how others were changed by responding to John's message of repentance. (Jesus is indirectly stating that rejection of John is rejection of Him.) As with the Sermon on the Mount, Jesus is emphasizing conduct over empty confession.

The Expositor's Bible Commentary notes that "The shock value of Jesus' statement can only be appreciated when the low esteem in which tax collectors were held, not to mention prostitutes, is taken into account. In our day of soft pornography on TV, we are not shocked by 'prostitutes.' But Jesus is saying that the scum of society, though it says no to God, repents, performs the Father's will, and enters the kingdom, whereas the religious authorities loudly say yes to God but never do what he says, and therefore they fail to enter. Their righteousness is not enough (Matt. 5:20). Thus the parable makes no distinction between Jew and Gentile but between religious leader and public sinner."[7]

THE PARABLE OF THE WICKED VINEDRESSERS

Jesus tells this parable to the people (Luke 20:9) about their religious leaders (Matt. 21:45). He exposes their attitude as that of an unwillingess to be accountable to the LORD God, not unlike Judah, similarly represented in Isaiah 5:1–7.

Read Matthew 21:33–46 and note the following. What does the landowner do when he has completed preparing his vineyard? (v. 33)

Absentee landlords were common in first-century Palestine. The unspoken allusion to Isaiah 5 makes the landowner a

God-figure, working through intermediaries like the Old Testament prophets.

How are the intermediaries treated by the vinedressers? (vv. 34–36)

How do the vinedressers treat the son? (vv. 37–39)

What results from this final rejection? (vv. 40–41) According to verse 43, who are the other vinedressers?

Nowhere in the Synoptics do we find the religious leaders saying, "Jesus is the Messiah; come, let's kill God's Son." Their actions are equivalent to this, however, bringing upon themselves God's wrath and the transference of their leadership to others (see Matt. 16:21; 17:23; Rom. 11:17–22).

How does Jesus support their self-condemning conclusion? (v. 42)

"Have you never read in the Scriptures. . . ?" is Jesus' way of saying the Old Testament points to Him (see Matt. 12:3; 19:4). The quote is from Psalm 118:22–23.

Jesus stands not only in God's premier place, but He is also identified how in verses 42 and 44?

Verses 42 and 44 allude to Isaiah 8:14–15 and Daniel 2:34, 44–45. Leon Morris explains their meaning: "To fall on the stone, or have the stone fall on one, in either case means destruction. People may reject and oppose Jesus but it is they, not he, who will suffer. The second part of the saying will refer to the future judgment. It will be their attitude to Jesus that will mean the final destruction of the people of his day."[8]

THE PARABLE OF THE WEDDING FEAST

This parable shows the contempt which Israel, especially her leaders, had for God's grace. It is similar to Jesus' parable of the Great Supper (Luke 14:15–24), questioning the confidence of those who, for one reason or another, take it for granted that they will be part of God's consummated kingdom.

Read Matthew 22:1–14 and note the following. What is the purpose of this parable? (v. 2)

How do the invited guests respond to the invitation? (vv. 3–6)

Those who were invited would have already received an invitation. First-century custom was to invite guests and then send a second invitation when the meal is ready. Jesus' reference is the religious leaders, not outsiders who have never even received a "first" invitation. Note their double refusal (v. 4).

What is the king's twofold response? (vv. 7–9)

Though the primary purpose of this parable is to teach what will be involved in the consummation of the kingdom, we must remember that the kingdom is already here and attracting both good and bad (those who repent and reflect kingdom righteousness and those who do not but claim to [v. 10; see Matt. 5:20; 13:47–53]).

What action does this attraction of both good and bad necessitate on the part of the king? (vv. 11–13)

R. T. France notes that "A *wedding garment* is not a special type of garment, but the clean clothes (preferably white) which would normally be worn on a special occasion; to come in dirty clothes is an insult to the host. Each guest was responsible for his own clothing. [The] lesson is that, though entry to God's salvation is free for all, it is not therefore without standards, or to be taken lightly. The warning that the new tenants must produce the fruit (Matt. 21:41, 43) is here reinforced. It was the claim to belong without an appropriate change of life which characterized the old Israel and brought about its rejection; the new people of God must not fall into the same error. The *garment* should probably not be pressed further than this. . . ."[9]

What is the concluding application of all three parables? (v. 14)

Jesus' parables further infuriate the impenitent scribes and chief priests. As the final Tuesday continues, "they sought to lay hands on Him, but feared the multitude . . . so they left Him and went away" (Mark 12:12). Meanwhile, "the Pharisees went and plotted how they might entangle Him in His talk" (Matt. 22:15), "in order to deliver Him to the power and the authority of the governor" (Luke 20:20). Their plan? Link up with the Herodians (Matt. 22:16) and send "spies who [pretend] to be righteous" (Luke 20:20). Jesus is unmoved, using the situation to give us some of His most famous instruction.

TRIBUTE TO CAESAR

Read Luke 20:20–26.

In their subterfuge plot, how do the chief priests and scribes try to be disarming? (v. 21)

"Teacher" is "an objective description (equivalent to 'rabbi') and indicates the societal rank and role of Jesus without prejudice to the personal attitude toward him of the one who uses the title (see Luke 5:5)."[10]

Why does Jesus answer their question with a question? (vv. 23–24)

"Craftiness" is "hypocrisy" in Mark's account (12:12) and "wickedness" in Matthew's (22:18). Mark and Matthew also add an additional question by Jesus, "Why do you test Me?" His opponents are seeking something by which to impress the Roman court (see Luke 23:2).

 WORD WEALTH

Craftiness, *panourgia,* means "versatile cleverness, astute knavery, sophisticated cunning, unscrupulous conduct, evil treachery, deceptive scheming, arrogant shrewdness, and sly arrogance. Used only five times in the New Testament, it refers to Satan's deceiving Eve (2 Cor. 11:3), the Pharisees' trying to trick Jesus (Luke 20:23), the deception of false teachers (Eph. 4:14), the self-entrapment of the worldly wise (1 Cor. 3:19), and the improper method of presenting the gospel (2 Cor. 4:2)."[11]

What are the implications of Jesus' answer (v. 25) in terms of defining the Christian response to the state? (see Rom. 13:1–7; 1 Pet. 2:13–17)

WHOSE WIFE DOES SHE BECOME?

A different segment of the Jewish leadership, the Sadducees, now question Jesus to make His promised resurrection look ridiculous.

Read Luke 20:27–40 and note the following. What tenet of the Sadducees' theology belies their question? (v. 27)

What is their alleged concern? (vv. 28–33)

Their argument is a device used in debate to make one's opponent appear absurd. "Try to untangle this knot in light of your foolish belief in the resurrection!" The popular belief of the day (even outside the Sadducees) was that marriage relationships continued in the age to come as they were before.

BEHIND THE SCENES

The Sadducees (v. 28) are pointing to the Mosaic provision of "Levirate Marriage" in Deuteronomy 25:5–10, with allusion to Genesis 38:8–10. "Levirate marriage [was] a form of marriage prescribed by the Law of Moses in which a man was required to marry the widow of a brother who died with no male heir. The term levirate means 'husband's brother.' The purpose of the law was to provide an heir for the dead brother, thereby preserving his name and estate. The law also was designed to provide for the welfare of the widows. The story of Ruth and Boaz, recorded in the Book of Ruth, is a good example of the levirate form of marriage."[12] The Sadducees' question is really pointless, since this provision was not practiced by the first century.

How does Jesus collapse their scheme? (vv. 34–35)

What makes resurrection life fundamentally different? (v. 36)

How does Jesus substantiate His theology? (vv. 37–38)

Who publicly acknowledges His answer? (v. 39)

The scribes here are apparently Pharisaic, believing in the resurrection.

THE GREATEST COMMANDMENT

The Pharisees' motive continues to be ugly ("a question, testing Him" [Matt. 22:35]), but Jesus yields a rich and positive answer.

Read Matthew 22:34–40 and note the following. Who asks the question? (v. 35)

"Lawyer" (Greek, *nomikos*) refers to a scribal expert in the Law. The test behind his question (v. 36) is that of trying to get Jesus to repudiate some of the commandments through a careless answer, which would validate their claim that He was destroying the Law (see Matt. 5:17).

What is the first and great commandment? (v. 37)

   BEHIND THE SCENES

To avoid the trap, Jesus talks about the principle behind the whole Law, quoting Deuteronomy 6:5, which is part of the *Shema'*. The *Shema'* ("Hear Thou") is a Jewish confession of faith that consists of three passages (Num. 15:37–41; Deut. 6:4–6; 11:13–21). It was prayed twice daily by pious Jews. Heart, soul, and mind seem to many to so overlap that we should not make too much of the distinctions. Jesus' intent is to show that people are to love the Lord (their) God with the totality of their being.

Quoting Leviticus 19:18, Jesus teaches that something is to follow on the heels of total devotion to the LORD God (v. 39). What is it?

In Leviticus, "neighbor" refers to fellow Israelites or resident aliens. Luke 10:29–37 expands the meaning to include anyone who needs help.

How does Jesus summarize the importance of these commandments? (v. 40)

"Hang" (Greek, *kremannumi*) is a technical term for laws derived from other laws. "Nothing in Scripture can cohere or be truly obeyed unless these two [laws] are observed. The entire biblical revelation demands heart religion marked by total allegiance to God, loving him and loving one's neighbor. Without these two commandments the Bible is sterile."[13]

Tuesday is not yet over. Before He leaves the temple for the final time, the Synoptists tell us Jesus (1) once again challenges the prevailing understanding of the nature and ministry of the awaited Davidic Messiah (Matt. 22:41–46); (2) warns against and pronounces woes upon the Pharisees (Matt. 23:1–36); (3) laments over Jerusalem (Luke 13:34–35; see Luke 19:41–44); and (4) reflects on the widow's two mites (Mark 12:41–44). He also delivers the famous Olivet Discourse (Matt. 24—25), where He goes nightly to lodge during the final week (Luke 21:37). He closes the day by telling His disciples that the day after tomorrow, Thursday evening, which is the beginning of Friday by Jewish reckoning, "the Son of Man will be delivered up to be crucified" (Matt. 26:2).

THE CONSPIRACY UNFOLDS

Wednesday is marked by an acceleration in the conspiracy to kill Jesus. Read Matthew 26:3–5, 14–16 and note the following. Who is involved in the final conspiracy and who's chairing it? (v. 3)

This is apparently a semiformal meeting of a subgroup within the Sanhedrin. France notes that "it is striking that the scribes and Pharisees . . . are not mentioned now that the time for official action has come. It is the priestly and aristocratic group who make the running. The official representatives of Israel . . . have now finally rejected the Messiah."[14] Caiaphas was high priest from A.D. 18–36.

What is their plan? (v. 4)

What is the obstacle they've yet to overcome? (v. 5)

How is their dilemma solved? (vv. 14–16; see Luke 22:6)

According to Luke 22:3, who is behind Judas's actions?

The fact that Satan entered Judas does not necessarily mean he's now a demoniac, unable to control his actions. Rather, Judas has opened the door to Satan, failing to resist his temptation. No doubt his thievery (John 12:6) opened the door for this. Regarding balancing the human role and the divine role behind the betrayal, Nolland notes, "Keeping in mind the wider Lukan narrative, one must not forget that this delivering up of Jesus, though a betrayal, at the same time fulfills the divine intention (see Acts 2:23) and is fully anticipated by Jesus himself (Luke 9:44; 22:21–22)."[15] None of this removes responsibility from Judas, who made his own choices and performed his own acts.

The Last Supper

It is now Thursday of the final week. In spite of the increasing threat on His life, Jesus remains in control and initiates sharing a final Passover meal with His disciples. He uses this longstanding Jewish celebration[16] to, among other things, institute Christianity's Eucharist. This is also the setting in which He washes His disciples' feet, an incident recorded only by John (13:1–20).

The event begins during the afternoon of "the Day of Unleavened Bread, when the Passover must be killed" (Luke 22:7). According to the Jewish calendar, this would be Nisan 14 between 2:30 P.M. and 6:00 P.M., the scheduled time for the Passover lamb to be slaughtered before sunset. (Nisan corresponds to most of our March and the beginning of April.) Nisan 14 had been called "the Day of Unleavened Bread" for centuries. Jewish families on this day searched their homes thoroughly and collected all leaven to burn by noon. They also prepared the unleavened loaves for the Passover meal (see Exod. 12:18–20).

Read Luke 22:7–13 and note the following. What are Jesus' instructions to Peter and John? (v. 8)

Jesus apparently wants to ensure privacy for this final, important event, which not only institutes the Eucharist but points to His perfect redemptive work.

How were Peter and John to know whom to contact for a place to house the group? (vv. 9–11)

A man carrying a pitcher of water would have been easy to locate, for it was customary that only women carried such pitchers. Jesus may have made the arrangements earlier in the week.

Where do they eat the Last Supper? (vv. 12–13)

"Upper room" indicates it is on the second story under a flat roof with an outside stairway. "Furnished" refers to the needed utensils and the couches on which they traditionally reclined to eat the Passover.

The meal begins after sunset (Nisan is begun at sunset; see Genesis 1:5, 8, 13).

Read Luke 22:14–30. Why is this meal important to Jesus? (vv. 15–16)

BEHIND THE SCENES

Jesus' statement in Luke 22:16 indicates that the evening has great symbolic significance. Reference to participation in the consummated kingdom is often portrayed through the language of a majestic banquet (see Rev. 19:1–10).

Norval Geldenhuys comments that "On the eve of His crucifixion Jesus knows that the whole course of His life of self-sacrifice and humiliation on earth is now drawing to an end. But He also knows that the day will come when He as the Triumphant One will lead His followers to the beautiful heritage of complete redemption and blessedness. This full blessedness which will commence with the end of the age has often been represented by the symbol of the celebration of a Messianic banquet. For this reason the Saviour here refers to the celebration of the feast on that coming day when the sovereign dominion of God has come to full revelation and the redemption wrought by the grace of God, as symbolized in the Passover celebrations, has become a blessed and perfect reality."[17]

What does Jesus then do? (vv. 17–19; see 1 Cor. 11:23–26)

The bread (v. 19) would have been thin because unleavened. It likely refers to the loaf which traditionally opened the main part of the Passover meal. The identity of the cup (v. 17) is less certain, as the meal has four different symbolic cups. It is best not to speculate on which of the four Jesus used. The church has never been able to agree on how far the implications of Jesus' statement, "This is My body" (v. 19) go. Protestants generally agree it means "represents" or "signifies" (see John 6:35; 8:12; 1 Cor. 10:4). Jesus' strong statement should not be watered down, but neither should it be taken literally. "Which is given for you" (v. 19) is a reference to the Crucifixion. In the Passover meal setting, with this statement Jesus adds a new dimension to the symbolism; Passover had always represented deliverance, but never vicarious sacrifice.

"Gave thanks" (v. 17) is translated from the Greek verb *eucharisteo*, from which we get Eucharist.

What is the primary purpose for Communion? (v. 19)

"In remembrance of Me" (v. 19) clearly indicates that Communion is primarily to direct our attention to the person of Christ and not simply the benefits we derive from partaking of it. Verse 18 suggests that we are to remember that He shall return to consummate the kingdom of God. What does Jesus do after the meal? (v. 20)

By making a new covenant, Jesus means that His death will open a new approach to the Eternal Living God, the LORD God of Israel, Creator of mankind. Thus, His sacrifice abolishes the old sacrificial system (see Jer. 31:31–34; Heb. 9:23–28).

What is revealed after the dramatic events of the meal? (vv. 21–23; see Matt. 26:25 for an additional detail)

What results from the apostles' search for the betrayer? (v. 24)

Jesus responds by redefining their concept of greatness. What is His definition? (vv. 25–27)

Though their dispute over greatness is not commendable, for what does Jesus commend them? (v. 28)

What does He confer on them and what will this privilege entail? (vv. 29–30)

"Kingdom" here refers to participation in His delegated royal rule now (see Luke 12:32), as well as in the consummation, where they will fulfill as yet undefined leadership roles.

 FAITH ALIVE

Do you enjoy celebrating the Lord's Supper? Do you feel you understand it enough to explain it to a new convert? Would you feel comfortable leading others in the Eucharist? Why or why not?

Do you approach Communion to first and foremost honor Him and to celebrate all His life, death, and resurrection? Knowing that the nature of God is to respond to heartfelt worship (see Ps. 22:3), do you come to the Table in faith to receive the life and blessings it symbolizes?

From this study, how can you deepen your participation in Communion?

Judas leaves at this point, and John records Jesus' famous teachings on the New Commandment, the Upper Room farewell discourses, and the climactic intercessory prayer (John 13—17). Then, "when they had sung a hymn, they went out to the Mount of Olives" (Mark 14:26).

Read Mark 14:27–31 and note the following. What issue does Jesus address that prompts the discussion about Peter's denial? (vv. 27–28)

How does Peter take this news? (v. 29)

What is Jesus' response to Peter's claim? (v. 30)

Does Peter then drop the issue? (v. 31)

Luke 22:31–32 adds the additional insight that the Cross will be used by Satan to try to prove they do not have the substance to maintain loyalty to Christ. Jesus warns them of this and notes He's praying for them. They will not come out unscathed. There will be denial (Zech. 13:7), but in the end their faith will not fail and they (especially Peter) will be a strength to others.

1. John Nolland, *Word Biblical Commentary: Luke* (Dallas: Word, 1989), 502.
2. *Spirit-Filled Life Bible* (Nashville: Thomas Nelson, 1991), 1531.
3. Ibid., 1553.
4. Frank E. Gaebelein, ed., *The Expositor's Bible Commentary*, Vol. 8 (Grand Rapids: Zondervan, 1984), 437.
5. *Spirit-Filled Life Bible*, notes on Matt. 21:8, 21:9.
6. William Lane, *The New International Commentary on the New Testament: Mark* (Grand Rapids: Eerdmans, 1974), 407.
7. Gaebelein, 450.
8. Leon Morris, *Tyndale New Testament Commentaries: Luke* (Grand Rapids: Eerdmans, 1990), 313.
9. R. T. France, *Tyndale New Testament Commentaries: Matthew* (Grand Rapids: Eerdmans, 1986), 313.
10. Nolland, *Luke*, 355.
11. *Spirit-Filled Life Bible*, 1723, "Word Wealth: 1 Cor. 3:19 craftiness."
12. *Nelson's Illustrated Bible Dictionary*, 644.
13. Gaebelein, 465.
14. France, *Matthew*, 361.
15. Nolland, *Luke*, 1031.
16. *Nelson's Illustrated Bible Dictionary*, 380–381.
17. Norval Geldenhuys, *The New International Commentary on the New Testament: Luke* (Grand Rapids: Eerdmans, 1979), 553–554.

Lesson 10/Then the End Will Come

Untold images come to mind when the subject is "the end of the world." And though the Bible has a lot to say about this, Christians disagree, sometimes strongly, about the interpretation of key prophetic elements in Scripture.

 WORD WEALTH

Eschatology, the study of the end times, comes from two Greek words, *eschatos*, meaning "extreme end," and *logia*, meaning "discussion." Because God not only reveals Himself to men, but also works redemptively in history, biblical eschatology is concerned with the destiny of both.

People ask many questions when trying to interpret prophecy. Do the prophecies have a dual fulfillment? What is meant to be interpreted literally, how much symbolically? How much, if any, has the church replaced physical Israel? Does the current nation of Israel have a place in God's prophetic plan? Will the church be raptured before, during, or after the Great Tribulation? Part of the difficulty in answering these and like questions is that biblical glimpses into the future come chiefly through two complex literary forms: the prophetic and the apocalyptic, both with symbolism that is at best difficult.

On Tuesday evening during the final week of His life, Jesus gave His most in-depth teaching about the end of the age. This happened during the Olivet Discourse, so named because Jesus spoke it "as He sat on the Mount of Olives opposite the temple" (Mark 13:3). Having established that the kingdom of God had come in Him, Jesus now establishes its consummation in the distant future, when this age will end and a new age will be inaugurated (Luke 19:11–27).

The following study is, of course, not an exhaustive look, but hopefully something to give us understanding of Jesus' main points.

THE DESTRUCTION OF THE TEMPLE

Read Matthew 24:1–2. What prompts the discussion? (see Luke 21:5)

What is Jesus' surprising response? (v. 2)

BEHIND THE SCENES

In Matthew 24:1–2 Jesus leaves the temple and walks to the Mount of Olives. R. T. France observes that "the fact that he goes to the Mount of Olives (v. 3) may be a further echo of Ezekiel 11:23, where 'the glory of the Lord,' on leaving the temple, stops at the same point. The disciples' preoccupation with *the buildings*, therefore, may be due . . . to incredulity that Jesus could be repudiating such a noble structure dedicated to the glory of God [which was] still in the process of completion."[1]

THE BEGINNING OF SORROWS

On the Mount of Olives the disciples came to Jesus privately, seeking clarification about the destruction of the temple (Matt. 24:3). But their question is twofold, going beyond the historical destruction of the temple. "Tell us, when will these things be? And what will be the sign of Your coming, and of the end of the age?" (Matt. 24:3). Jesus' answer seems to intertwine the historical destruction of Jerusalem (by the Romans in A.D. 70) with future events about the Second Coming and the final events of this present age.

Jesus begins by warning His disciples not to jump to conclusions about the destruction of the temple *or* about the Second Coming (Matt. 24:4). Read Matthew 24:3–22. What is Jesus' first warning? (vv. 4–5)

The 30-plus years prior to the temple's destruction and the time before the end of this age will be characterized by what events? (vv. 6, 7)

How are disciples to respond to such events, and what are they *not* to conclude? (v. 6)

How are these tumults to be viewed, whether with reference to the time prior to the destruction of the temple or prior to Jesus' return? (v. 8)

What can Jesus' disciples expect during this age? (v. 9)

What, unfortunately, will happen to some disciples because of persecution? (vv. 10–12)

Persecution and the death of many of Jesus' disciples are part of the whole history of the church, beginning with the 40 years between the Ascension and the destruction of the Temple. No wonder "the souls of those who had been slain for the word of God and the testimony which they held" cry out for God to quickly close this age (Rev. 6:9–11).

What must God's Spirit develop in disciples to withstand the difficulties of this age? (v. 13)

"The end" here does not refer to the apocalyptic end. It is a standard biblical phrase for "right through one's life."

WORD WEALTH

Endures, *hupomeno*, means "to hold one's ground in conflict, bear up against adversity, hold out under stress, stand firm, persevere under pressure, wait calmly and courageously. It is not passive resignation to fate and mere patience, but the active, energetic resistance to defeat that allows calm and brave endurance."[2]

On the positive side, what is to occur during the extended Time of Sorrows? (v. 14; see Matthew 28:16–20 for Jesus' elaboration of the Great Commission.)

It is unbiblical to use Jesus' words here to calculate the time of the end. All He means is that neither the destruction of the temple nor the end of the age can come until the gospel has reached far outside the nation of Israel. This began during the church's first generation and continues today.

PROBING THE DEPTHS

Sorrows (Greek, *odines*) means "woes" and is used in the Old Testament of the pains of birth (see Is. 26:17). George Ladd explains the history and significance of this expression: "The Old Testament speaks of the birth of a nation through a period of woes (Is. 66:8; Jer. 22:23; Hos. 13:13; Mic. 4:9), and from these verses there arose in Judaism the idea that the messianic Kingdom must emerge from a period of suffering that was called the messianic woes or 'the birth pangs of the Messiah.'"[3] Jesus therefore sees the era of "the birth pangs of the Messiah" (the beginning of sorrows) as referring to the church age. The tumultuous signs of Matthew 24 therefore characterize the entire life of the church, from the Ascension to the Second Coming, and find intensification as the end draws closer (Rev. 6:1–8). Many scholars believe John describes "the beginning of sorrows" more definitively in the breaking of the six seals (Rev. 6:1–17).[4]

Within the general time frame of "the beginning of sorrows," Matthew, Mark, and Luke turn their attention to the historical fall of Jerusalem and the temple (Matt. 24:15–22; Mark 13:14–20; Luke 21:20–24).

Read Matthew 24:15–22 and Luke 21:20–24. According to Luke 21:20, what might be meant by Matthew 24:15 "when you see the 'abomination of desolation,' spoken of by Daniel the prophet, standing in the holy place"?

What are people to do when they see the abomination of desolation, or Jerusalem surrounded by armies? (Matt. 24:16–18)

For what are the disciples to pray? (Matt. 24:20)

How great is the siege against Jerusalem, and what brings it to an end? (Matt. 24:21–22)

Jesus' statement is to be evaluated in light of the fact that there has "never [been] so high a percentage of a great city's population so thoroughly and painfully exterminated and enslaved as during the Fall of Jerusalem."[5] "Nor ever shall be" would thus obviously not be a reference to the intense destruction of the global Great Tribulation and time of God's wrath (Rev. 8:7—9:21), which biblically stand by themselves as part of the unique period of events of the end of all things after the present world is over.

 PROBING THE DEPTHS

The "abomination of desolation" (Matt. 24:15) comes from Daniel 9:27, 11:31, and 12:11. An "abomination" in the Old Testament is any type of idolatrous affront to the worship of the LORD God. Initially, according to Alan Cole, Daniel's prophecy "probably referred to the statue set up in the temple by Antiochus [167 B.C.], so profaning it, and the sacrifice of swine's flesh on the altar. In this passage, it fairly certainly refers to the encirclement of Jerusalem by Roman armies. The Roman 'eagles,' the standards of the legions, were held by the Zealots to be sacrilegious 'abominations,' being 'idols,' and as such forbidden in the Ten Commandments. In A.D. 70, Roman standards, often bearing images of Caesar, stood on the site of the ruined temple."[6]

Prophecy often "foreshortens" history through what is called a "two-dimensional" fulfillment—both an immediate historical fulfillment and a long-range, unspecified future fulfillment (see Matt. 1:23 as an expanded fulfillment of Is. 7:14). Cole continues "Here God's immediate judgment on His people at one particular point in history is almost imperceptibly dovetailed into His universal judgment on all humanity at the last day."[7] Hence, the "abomination of desolation" has a secondary reference to the Antichrist. "Standing in the holy place" probably means he will demand the worship of men (2 Thess. 2:3–4; Rev. 13:1–10). Both Antiochus and the Roman armies therefore prefigure the Antichrist.

EVENTS OF THE END

Though scholars vary at this point, it is generally conceded that Matthew 24:23 (see Mark 13:21) marks the beginning of the series of events of the end. Matthew 24:23–28, then, is a shortened version of the Great Tribulation (Rev. 8:7–19). The era of "the beginning of sorrows" has ended.

Read Matthew 24:23–28 and note the following. What will significantly mark the Great Tribulation and why? (vv. 23–24; see v. 5)

What is to be the church's response to the Great Tribulation temptation? (vv. 25–26)

Jesus' return will not be a secret affair that one could miss. What will it be like? (vv. 27–28)

THE COMING OF THE SON OF MAN

PROBING THE DEPTHS

The Son of Man is Jesus' favorite self-designation. Jesus uses it to highlight His humanness, and to show that He speaks and acts as God's representative man. Based on Dan. 7:13, this title "involves the claim to be a pre-existent heavenly kind of messiah who has unexpectedly appeared as a man among men."[8]

Read Matt. 24:29–35. What will immediately precede Christ's return? (v. 29)

Details of this verse are difficult, as it draws on extensive Old Testament apocalyptic imagery. Scholars therefore differ as to its significance and literalness. It either symbolically describes the great political stirrings and judgments of God just prior to Christ's return (see Is. 13:10; 24:23), or it describes the fact that Christ's return will be marked by great cosmic events. The latter seems most likely, yet we are wise to remain non-dogmatic here.

How will Christ return (see Dan. 7:13–14; Rev. 19:11–16), and how will the unredeemed respond to the Second Coming? (v. 30; see Zech. 12:10–12; Rev. 1:7)

What will accompany His return? (v. 31)

This is equivalent to what is commonly termed the Rapture (1 Thess. 4:17); happening in conjunction with the Second Coming of Christ (Rev. 19:11–16), it will immediately follow the resurrection of the dead saints (not mentioned in Matthew). It is this writer's belief that all this is clearly after "the time of sorrows and the [Great] tribulation of those days" (Matt. 24:3–28). If you differ, express your conviction here.

THE PARABLE OF THE FIG TREE

Jesus now illustrates what He's been teaching with a countryman's parable. Some see the fig tree as symbolic of Israel, though others disagree and say He could have used any tree to make His point.

Read Mark 13:28–31. What do you think the "tender branch" and spring "leaves" on a "fig tree" symbolize? (v. 28)

What do you think the time of birth pains and the Great Tribulation symbolize? (v. 29)

How does Jesus teach that the events of Jerusalem's fall are inextricably woven into the final events of this age? (v. 30)

Through all the upheavals of this age and the events of the end, what can be counted on as steady and permanent? (v. 31)

IN THE MEANTIME . . .

Although we are to know generally about the nature of this age and the overall events of the end and are to be convinced of the surety of the Second Coming, we are morally bound to resist all temptation to try to know what only the Father knows: the exact time of the Second Coming. "But of that day and hour no one knows, not even the angels of heaven, nor the Son, but only the Father" (Mark 13:32; see Acts 1:7). Never presume to accurately calculate Jesus' return. It will be more unexpected than any of us likely realizes (Matt. 24:36–44). The fact that we cannot know the date does not mean we cannot be prepared. We can prepare by praying for strength to maintain a life of vigilant obedience to God (Luke 21:36). Any "faithful and wise servant" would do this (Matt. 24:45–51).

In Matthew's account, the Olivet Discourse expands the need of vigilance with two parables. One reinforces Jesus' call to constant readiness (25:1–13). One gives further definition to what maintaining readiness entails (25:14–30).

The Parable of the Wise and Foolish Virgins

This parable is fashioned after the Old Testament idea of the Messiah as bridegroom (see Is. 54:4–6; Ezek. 16:7–34), which was already applied to Jesus by John the Baptist (John 3:27–30) and by Jesus Himself (Matt. 9:15).

Read Matthew 25:1–13 and note the following. Who are the main characters of the parable? (v. 1)

Why are five of the virgins wise and five foolish? (vv. 3–5)

Can preparedness for the Lord's return be transferred or shared? (vv. 6–9)

What happens to the foolish virgins? (vv. 10–12)

What is Jesus' conclusion? (v. 13)

This parable complements the apostle Paul's teaching that no person is saved by works; nevertheless true discipleship requires more than mere words. Disciples reveal their faith by a lifestyle of obedience and vigilant service in the power of the Holy Spirit (see Matt. 7:22–23).

The Parable of the Talents

The Parable of the Talents (Matt. 25:14–30) goes beyond that of the virgins by defining readiness. France defines "readiness" here not as "a matter of passively 'waiting,' but of responsible activity, producing results which the coming 'master' can see and approve. For the period of waiting was not intended to be an empty, meaningless 'delay,' but a period of opportunity to put to good use the 'talents' entrusted to his 'slaves.'"[9] Though different in detail, it makes essentially the same point as the Parable of the Minas (Luke 19:12–27).

Read Matthew 25:14–30 and note the following. Who are the main characters? (v. 14)

How does the man determine how much of his goods each servant will receive? (v. 15)

"Talents" (Greek, *talanta*) here does not refer to abilities people possess. Instead it is a unit of exchange, which later became a coin. In the parable, talents represent unspecified opportunities for service in the kingdom of God.

What two responses to opportunities are noted? (vv. 16–18)

What does the man do when he returns from his travel? (v. 19)

"After a long time" suggests the Second Coming will be long delayed.

Why are two of the servants commended? (vv. 20–23)

What is the response of the third servant and why? (vv. 24–25)

"A hard man" has the idea of a person who exploits his servants.

What is the man's response? (vv. 26–30)

Readiness is not merely a matter of keeping one's slate clean; it involves active, responsible service producing results.

Verse 30 "need not be concluded as referring to the loss of one's justification, but may instead portray the forfeiting of one's reward for committed service in the kingdom, a loss of joy, with weeping and gnashing one's teeth, reflecting the remorse for lost opportunity."[10]

 FAITH ALIVE

Do you see yourself as highly motivated to kingdom service? If not, why?

What specifically are you doing that would affirm Jesus' words, "Well done, good and faithful servant"?

Are you serving out of love, fear, or obligation?

Jesus closes the Olivet Discourse (Matt. 25:31–46) by teaching that the basis of the ultimate judgment of all the nations will be their response to His disciples. It reflects the same general theme and tone as that taught in Matthew 10:40–42.

1. R. T. France, *Tyndale New Testament Commentaries: Matthew* (Grand Rapids: Eerdmans, 1986), 336.
2. *Spirit-Filled Life Bible*, 1451, "Word Wealth: Matt. 24:13 endures."
3. George Ladd, *A Theology of the New Testament* (Grand Rapids: Eerdmans, 1974), 201–202.
4. The end of "the beginning of sorrows" is the seventh seal (Rev. 8:1) when the scroll (Rev. 5:1) of end-time events for the Great Tribulation is finally opened. Because the content of the seventh seal is a series of events, John describes the end of "the beginning of sorrows" with the sixth seal.
5. Frank E. Gaebelein, ed., *The Expositor's Bible Commentary* (Grand Rapids: Zondervan, 1984), 501.
6. R. Alan Cole, *Tyndale New Testament Commentaries: Mark* (Grand Rapids: Eerdmans, 1989), 277.
7. Ibid., 278–279.
8. Ladd, *New Testament*, 152.
9. France, *Matthew*, 352.
10. *Spirit-Filled Life Bible*, 1455, note on Matthew 25:30.

Lesson 11/From Gethsemane to the Cross

Late Thursday evening, having completed the important events of the Upper Room, Jesus and the eleven sing a hymn and go to the Mount of Olives where the events culminating in the Crucifixion begin (Mark 14:26).

In less than twenty-four hours, Jesus Christ will be crucified. The most significant event in history (in conjunction with the Resurrection) will unfold, forever changing how people can relate to God. Before the Crucifixion, however, several key events must come to pass: Gethsemane, the arrest, the High Priest's and Sanhedrin's interrogations, Peter's denial, Pilate's questioning of Jesus, Judas's suicide, Herod's questioning of Jesus, the crowd's cry for Barabbas, Pilate's giving Jesus to the Roman soldiers, the scourging, and the painful walk to Calvary. It is an unprecedented night and day.

We begin in Gethsemane (Hebrew for "oil-press"), an enclosed olive orchard on the slopes of the Mount of Olives (Luke 22:39), which John calls a garden (John 18:1). Jesus and the Twelve had met here many times before (John 18:2), but this night Jesus Christ "offered up prayers and supplications, with vehement cries and tears to Him who was able to save Him from death, and was heard because of His godly fear, though He was a Son, yet He learned obedience by the things which He suffered" (Heb. 5:7–8).

GETHSEMANE

Concerning Mark 14:32–42, R. T. France comments that "This remarkable narrative, which probably lies behind John

12:23–28 and Hebrews 5:7–10 as well as the explicit Synoptic accounts, gives perhaps the most intimate insight into the nature of Jesus' relationship with his Father, as well as into the cost of his Messianic mission. It blends together the reality of his humanity with the uniqueness of his position as Son of God. At the same time it illustrates the weakness of the disciples, and prepares us for their subsequent failure."[1]

Read Mark 14:32–42 and note the following. What is His instruction to the eight whom He leaves just inside the garden gate? (v. 32; see Luke 22:40)

What is His instruction to the three who go further into the garden with Him? (v. 34)

What is Jesus' spiritual and emotional state at this time? (vv. 33–34)

"Troubled and deeply distressed" together "describe an extremely acute emotion, a compound of bewilderment, fear, uncertainty and anxiety, nowhere else portrayed in such vivid terms as here."[2] "My soul is exceedingly sorrowful" is a reference to Psalm 42:5–6.

What is Jesus' first request in prayer? (v. 35)

Prostration in prayer usually indicates spiritual anguish (see Num. 16:22). The more normal biblical posture was standing with uplifted hands (see Mark 11:25).

As a sign of intimate, obedient surrender and unconditional confidence in His Father, how does Jesus address God? (v. 36)

As a human being, what is His first request? How does His second request express this obedience as the Son? (v. 36)

Jesus is exploring the limits of God's will, but never desiring to break outside of it. "This cup" refers to the wrath of God which He knows His crucifixion will entail (see Mark 10:38–39; 15:34; 2 Cor. 5:21).

Even in His agony, He is concerned about the three disciples with Him. He returns and finds them in what condition? (v. 37)

What does He reiterate to them? (v. 38)

"Temptation" (Greek, *peirasmos*) refers to a trial that entices one to be untrue to God. Behind such enticements are often demonic forces (see Mark 1:12–13), who often use physical weaknesses and limitations ("the flesh is weak") to lure disciples into wrong spiritual choices ("the spirit is willing").

How many times is this scene repeated? (vv. 39–41) What is His response the third time? (vv. 41–42)

 FAITH ALIVE

Successful Christian living results from knowing God's will and doing it by grace through faith. Have you determined to know as much of God's Word as you can? By what means do you now take in God's Word?

How about your preference for God's will over your own? Can you name an area or two in which you must honestly admit you're struggling with God's will?

How is the struggle manifesting itself?

With what mature Christian can you share your struggle, asking not only for prayer, but to be held accountable on a course of action that will see you yield to God's will?

THE ARREST

Judas knew where Jesus would be and led those who arrested Him to Gethsemane. The shocking fulfillment of Jesus' words, "Assuredly, I say to you, one of you will betray Me" (Matt. 26:21), is seen in Matthew's description of Judas as "one of the twelve" (26:47).

Read Matthew 26:47–56. Who comes with Judas and with what do they come? (v. 47)

How does Judas greet Jesus? (v. 49)

 BEHIND THE SCENES

R. T. France provides an enlightening note: "For a Rabbi's disciple to *kiss* his master (on hand or foot) was not an everyday greeting, but a mark of special honor. Nor dare the disciple take this initiative uninvited; to do so was a 'studied insult.' The greeting of Jesus as *Rabbi* in this context is therefore heavily ironical (see Matthew 26:25, the only other use of this address in Matthew, again by Judas). Judas's [self-initiated] action thus not only identifies Jesus to the arresting party, but marks his own public repudiation of Jesus' authority."[3]

What is Jesus' response to the betrayal? (v. 50)

Scholars vary as to whether Jesus' response is a question or a statement. The original Greek text was not punctuated. Likely, He is making a statement rather than asking a question, since He is fully aware of Judas's errand.

What is Peter's response? (v. 51)

What is Jesus' response to Peter's sincere yet impetuous action? (vv. 52–54; see Luke 22:51)

Jesus' statement in verse 52 "should be interpreted in its context, and not as a general endorsement of pacifism. He was laying down His life in fulfillment of the Scriptures."[4] A legion consisted of 6,000 soldiers.

What is Jesus' explanation of the situation? (v. 56)

"The Scriptures of the prophets" simply means the Old Testament (see Mark 14:49).

In fulfillment of Zechariah 13:7, what is the disciples' reaction when Jesus is bound to be led away? (v. 56)

Mark 14:51–52 adds the detail that "a certain young man," a disciple whom tradition says is Mark himself, is also there, wearing only a linen cloth (the customary outer garment, indicating he dressed hastily to get to the scene). He too flees, further emphasizing Jesus is forsaken by *all*.

JESUS BEFORE THE HIGH PRIEST

Read Matthew 26:59–66 and Mark 14:55–64. Late Thursday night, early Friday morning Jesus is led from Gethsemane "to Caiaphas the high priest, where the scribes and the elders were assembled" (Matt. 26:57). What is their first plan of attack? (Matt. 26:59–62)

What is the high priest's first line of interrogation, and what is Jesus' response? (Mark 14:60–62)

This is no casual question, but a solemn one asked "under oath by the living God" (Matt. 26:63). Jesus' response, "I am," is an allusion to God's revelation to Moses (Ex. 3:14). He thus puts Himself on an equality with the LORD God.

What is the high priest's response to Jesus' answer? (Mark 14:63–64)

PETER'S DENIAL

Read Luke 22:54–65. The spotlight momentarily shifts to Peter in fulfillment of Jesus' words at the Last Supper (Luke 22:31–34). Having fled when Jesus was bound and led away, Peter "followed at a distance" until the courtyard of the high priest's house (Luke 22:54). John asks the woman guarding the courtyard gate to let Peter in (John 18:15–16).

Read Luke 22:54–65 and note the following. What does Peter do upon entrance to the courtyard and how is he identified? (vv. 55–56)

What is his reaction to the servant girl's identification? (v. 57)

What happens in the course of the next hour or two? (vv. 58–60; see Mark 14:71)

What is Jesus' reaction to the third denial? (v. 61)

What is the impact of all this on Peter? (vv. 61–62; see v. 32)

What does Jesus experience for the remainder of the night? (vv. 63–65)

The guards are whiling away the night hours at Jesus' expense. Their cruel jokes are nothing short of blasphemy, but Jesus makes no response. He is clearly the Victim "who, when He was reviled, did not revile in return" (1 Pet. 2:23).

Friday at sunrise the chief priests held a consultation with the elders and scribes and the whole council (Mark 15:1). Their decision? They bound Jesus, led Him away, and delivered Him to Pilate (Mark 15:1).

 BEHIND THE SCENES

"The council" is the Sanhedrin or Jewish Supreme Court, "the highest ecclesiastical and political body among the Jews. The origin of this body is obscure. Jewish tradition speaks of two Sanhedrins. (1) The Little Sanhedrin had twenty-three members and judged cases other than those reserved for the highest body. (2) The Sanhedrin in Jerusalem was generally referred to as the Great Sanhedrin. It had seventy-one members, called 'elders,' who usually were chosen from among the chief priests and the scribes. The Sanhedrin was led by a president. The high priest, Caiaphas, seems to have been the presiding officer during the trial of Jesus, but this does not mean that the high priest was generally the president. Any decisions it made were binding. In cases involving life or death, the younger members voted first so they could not be influenced by their elders. No fewer than twenty-three members had to be present when such a case arose. If a verdict was reached by a majority of one, the number of court members had to be increased. Only when the full court was in session could a person be declared guilty by a majority of one."[5]

JESUS BEFORE PILATE AND HEROD

John Nolland explains that "With the ammunition that they think they will need, the Sanhedrin members move as a block to the court of Pilate in order to deliver Jesus into the hands of Roman 'justice.' By distorting elements of his teaching and presenting a politicized version of messiahship, they press their claim that Jesus is seeking to lead the Jewish nation away from its proper loyalty to Caesar. Pilate is skeptical, but they are vehement."[6]

Read Luke 23:1–5 and note the following. What are the trumped-up charges before Pilate? (v. 2)

The Romans had denied the Jews the right to execute capital punishment. This would have to come from Rome. Pontius Pilate ruled as procurator of Judea from A.D. 26–36. He had absolute authority over the non-Roman citizens in his province. He was responsible to the Roman governor who ruled from Syria to the north.

What is Pilate's response? (v. 3)

Pilate's "the King of the Jews" is to be understood as referring to a purely secular, political king. Jesus' covert answer is due to the fact that He is the Jews' messianic King, a matter He does not want to take up with Pilate.

Pilate is skeptical of the charges (v. 4). Using half-truths, what does the Sanhedrin then do? (v. 5)

Read Luke 23:6–12. What is Pilate's recourse? (vv. 6–7; see John 19:8)

What is Herod's initial response? (v. 8)

What is Jesus' response to Herod's interrogation? (v. 9)

"He answered him nothing" is not to be seen as rebellion or lack of cooperation. Jesus simply will not stoop to defend Himself against the false accusations. It is also a fulfillment of Isaiah 53:7; having settled the issue in Gethsemane, Jesus accepts God's will.

We know Herod has wanted to kill Jesus for some time (Luke 13:31). We are not told why he passes up the opportunity here. How does he vent his hostility? (v. 11)

What results from Pilate's shrewd move in sending Jesus to Herod? (v. 12)

Read Luke 23:13–25. What is Pilate's analysis of the situation? (vv. 13–16; see Matt. 27:19)

This is the second time Pilate declares Jesus' innocence. He proposes a concession, an educative beating and a release, in keeping with the fact that "at the feast he was accustomed to releasing one prisoner to them, whomever they requested . . . [and] he knew that the chief priests had handed Him over because of envy" (Mark 15:6, 10).

The people (v. 13), who have been somewhat of a buffer between Jesus and the Jewish leaders, are now summoned on the scene. What is their response to Pilate's concession? (vv. 18–19)

The referenced "rebellion" is likely some previous Zealot insurrection.

The protest intensifies to what demand? (v. 20–21)

In spite of Pilate's third declaration of Jesus' innocence, what finally prevails? (vv. 23–25; Matt. 27:24–25)

What does Pilate have done to Jesus before releasing Him to be crucified? (Matt. 27:27–31)

BEHIND THE SCENES

The Praetorium was the governor's official residence. The garrison may have numbered as many as 600 men. The scarlet robe was a soldier's red cape, used to imitate the emperor's purple robe. The crown of thorns and the reed were probably meant to mock Jewish royalty. And that Jesus is allowed His own clothes as He is led away to be crucified is unusual. "Criminals were normally led out naked for crucifixion. Perhaps the return of Jesus' *own clothes* was a regular concession to Jewish sensibility, which found nakedness offensive."[7]

THE CRUCIFIXION

The will of the clamoring people, which in a strange paradox is simultaneously the will of God (Acts 3:18), prevails. Jesus' fate has been determined by the Jewish leaders and people; the Roman authorities implement their will.

Read Luke 23:26–49 and note the following. Who actually carries Christ's cross most of the way? (v. 26; see John 19:17)

This unusual concession may have been allowed due to Jesus' extreme weakness from the Roman beating.

What is the response of some of the Jewish women to this event? (v. 27)

What does Jesus tell them? (vv. 28–31)

Jesus wants their repentance, not their sympathy. It is Israel who is actually facing the worse crisis. Luke 23:30 is a reference to Hosea 10:8 and likely represents a request to be hidden from the unspecified, impending destruction. Verse 31 is an obscure proverbial saying expressing "the inevitability and the scale of the judgment to fall."[8]

Who is crucified with Jesus? (v. 32)

The Crucifixion occurs at "a place called Golgotha, that is to say, Place of a Skull" (Matt. 27:33). This prominent public place outside Jerusalem (perhaps named for the shape of the area) was regularly known for its executions. Luke refers to it by its Latin name, Calvary ("a skull" [Luke 23:33]), rather than its Hebrew name, Golgotha.

What is Jesus offered after being fastened to the Cross? (Matt. 27:34)

"Victims to be executed customarily received wine drugged with myrrh to dull the senses (see Prov. 31:6). Jesus' refusal not only reflects His prayer (Matt. 26:39, 41, 42), but His will to avoid nothing of the cup given to Him by the Father."[9]

What is Jesus' concern while being crucified? (Luke 23:34)

What do the Roman soldiers do with His garments, and what is its significance? (Matt. 27:35)

Though allowed clothing earlier, Jesus is here stripped, His clothing considered the property of the executioners. We do not know if, as a Jew, He was permitted a loin cloth.

What time is it? (Mark 15:25)

"The third hour" was 9:00 A.M.

What is the reaction of many of the Jews, including the Jewish leaders? (Luke 23:35; see Mark 15:29)

Besides watching over Him to prevent any interference or rescue attempt (Matt. 27:36), what do the soldiers do after taking His garments? (Luke 23:36–37)

What public notice is posted as a deterrent to any such future crimes? (Luke 23:28; see John 19:19–22)

What is the attitude of the criminals who are crucified with Him? (Luke 23:39–41)

What does one of the criminals request? (Luke 23:42)

The first criminal mocks Jesus' royal claims; the second acknowledges Jesus' royal status with God and appeals for clemency. "When You come into Your kingdom" means, "When You pass from death into the place of exaltation at God's right hand."

How does Jesus respond? (Luke 23:43)

WORD WEALTH

Paradise, *paradeisos*, is borrowed from an old Persian word meaning "an enclosed space." In the Greek translation of the Old Testament it is used for the Garden of Eden (Gen. 2:8). It came to refer to the abode of God's people in the age to come.

It is now noon (Matt. 27:45). Jesus has committed his mother into John's care (John 19:25–27), and three hours of darkness come upon the land (Luke 23:44–45). The darkness probably symbolizes the satanic forces behind the cruel deed and that God has "forsaken" Jesus.

What happens at 3:00 P.M.? (Matt. 27:46)

One of the most profound verses in the Bible is Mark 15:34: "And at the ninth hour Jesus cried out with a loud voice, saying, *'Eloi, Eloi, lama sabachthani?'* which is trans-lated, 'My God, My God, why have You forsaken Me?'" This is also the only saying from the cross recorded by Mark.

PROBING THE DEPTHS

In Mark 15:34, Jesus quotes Psalm 22:1. We must not blunt the sharp edge of this cry. It is real, and it is, in Lane's words, "the inevitable sequel to the horror [Jesus] experienced in the Garden of Gethsemane. In . . . identifying Himself completely with sinners . . . Jesus . . . experienced the full alienation from God which the judgment He had assumed entailed. His cry expresses the profound horror of separation from God. The cry has a ruthless authenticity [to it]. Yet Jesus did not die renouncing God. Even in . . . His abandonment . . . He . . . expressed . . . a cry of affirmation, 'My God, My God.' "[10]

Hearing the "Eloi, Eloi" what do some think He's saying? (Mark 15:35)

What does one of the crowd then do? (Mark 15:36)

The sour wine here is wine vinegar diluted with water; it was a common, refreshing drink for laborers and soldiers. It is likely offered by the unidentified "someone" as an act of kindness, to which others in the crowd mockingly object. If he is to be relieved, let Elijah (commonly thought to be the Messiah's forerunner and helper) come and help Him.

After six hours on the Cross, what is Jesus' fifth recorded saying? (Luke 23:46)

What phenomena accompany His death? (Matt. 27:51–53)

The tearing of the temple's veil (likely the veil separating off the "Holy of Holies") symbolizes the opening of direct access to God through the provision of the Cross (see Heb. 6:19–20; 10:19–20). The resurrection of "many bodies of the saints" is a difficult portion of Scripture because of the unanswered questions it poses. Its essence, however, is clear: a uniquely symbolic foreshadowing of the resurrection of God's people.

AT A GLANCE

The Seven Words from the Cross	
In the four Gospels, a total of seven sayings are recorded from the cross.	
1. "Father, forgive them, for they do not know what they do."	Luke 23:34
2. "Assuredly, I say to you, today you will be with Me in Paradise."	Luke 23:43
3. "Woman, behold your son! Behold your mother."	John 19:26-27
4. "Eloi, Eloi, lama sabachthani?"	Mark 15:34
5. "Father, 'into Your hands I commit My spirit.'"	Luke 23:46
6. "I thirst."	John 19:28
7. "It is finished!"	John 19:30

THE DEATH OF JESUS (John 18, 19)[11]		
The world viewed Jesus' death as a scandal and as foolishness (1 Cor. 1:18–25). The early believers understood His death as fulfillment of Old Testament prophecy.	**Aspect of Jesus' Death**	**Old Testament Reference**
	In obedience to His Father (18:11)	Psalm 40:8
	Announced by Himself (18:32, see 3:14)	Numbers 21:8, 9
	In the place of His people (18:14)	Isaiah 53:4–6
	With evildoers (19:18)	Isaiah 53:12
	In innocence (19:6)	Isaiah 53:9
	Crucified (19:18)	Psalm 22:16
	Buried in a rich man's tomb (19:38–42)	Isaiah 53:9

1. R. T. France, *Tyndale New Testament Commentaries: Matthew* (Grand Rapids: Eerdmans, 1986), 372.
2. Frank E. Gaebelein, ed., *The Expositor's Bible Commentary* (Grand Rapids: Zondervan, 1984), 763.
3. France, *Matthew*, 375.
4. *Spirit-Filled Life Bible*, 1458, note on Matt. 26:52.
5. *Harper Study Bible* (Grand Rapids: Zondervan, 1991), note on Matt. 26:59. Used by permission.
6. John Nolland, *Word Biblical Commentary: Luke* (Dallas: Word, 1989), 1119.
7. France, *Matthew*, 394.
8. Nolland, *Luke*, 1138.
9. *Spirit-Filled Life Bible*, 1461, note on Matt. 27:34.
10. William Lane, *The New International Commentary on the New Testament: Mark* (Grand Rapids: Eerdmans, 1974), 572–573.
11. *Spirit-Filled Life Bible*, 1612, chart on "The Death of Jesus."

Lesson 12/God Raised Him Up

The New Testament is clear that "if Christ is not risen, your faith is futile; you are still in your sins!" (1 Cor. 15:17). Good Friday and Easter are inseparable. Easter is the day when weeping hearts and dashed hopes gave way to holy awe and great joy as Jesus met them, saying, "Rejoice!" (Matt. 28:9).

The focus of our final study in the Synoptics will be Jesus' burial, the guarded tomb, the Resurrection, various post-resurrection appearances, Jesus' final words, and the Ascension.

THE BURIAL

Jesus died about 3:00 on Friday afternoon, and Jewish law required that a crucified body be removed from its cross before the start of the Sabbath at sundown. In order to hasten death (by asphyxiation) of the three crucified on Golgotha, "the Jews asked Pilate that their legs might be broken, and that they might be taken away (John 19:31). When the soldiers came to Jesus (having broken the legs of the two criminals), they saw that He was already dead, so they did not break His legs (John 19:32). Instead, they confirm His death by piercing His side. Both these actions were prophetic fulfillments (John 19:34–37).

Read Mark 15:42–47 and note the following. Who asks Pilate for Jesus' body? (v. 43; see Matt. 27:57; Luke 23:50–51)

What is Pilate's initial response? (v. 44)

Pilate is surprised because men sometimes lingered for days before dying of exposure, thirst, or asphyxiation from the hanging position's impact on the respiratory system.

What does Joseph do with Christ's body? (v. 46)

The body was placed hastily in the tomb due to the late hour. The embalming process was completed after the Sabbath (Mark 16:1). The fine linen is a gauze shroud.

How is the tomb sealed? (v. 46)

Read Matthew 27:62–66 and note the following. What do the chief priests and Pharisees think of Jesus? (v. 63)

What is their concern? (v. 63)

What is their request to Pilate? (v. 64)

WORD WEALTH

Deception, *plane*, originally meant "a wandering; hence, the English word 'planet.' Metaphorically, the word denotes a going astray, an error. In the New Testament the straying is always in respect to morals and doctrine."[1]

What is Pilate's response and the leaders' subsequent action? (vv. 65–66)

Pilate's answer is best seen as cynical, no doubt from being weary of the whole matter of Jesus Christ of Nazareth. "You have a guard" probably means they have temple guards whom they are free to use; this accounts for the guards later reporting to the chief priests (Matt. 28:11).

THE RESURRECTION

R. T. France observes that "the New Testament nowhere describes Jesus' resurrection. All we are given is an account of its effects, from two points of view: the tomb was found to be empty, and the disciples met the risen Lord. . . . The emphasis throughout (except in the story of the guard) is not on factual proof for the non-Christian world, but on the impact of the incredible truth on Jesus' bewildered and exhilarated followers, on their fear and joy, doubt and assurance. It is with the restoration of their broken relationship with him, with all that this implies for their continuing mission, that Matthew will conclude his book."[2]

 ## PROBING THE DEPTHS

The Synoptics indicate exactly where Jesus' spirit/soul were between the Cross and the Resurrection. From His words to the penitent criminal (Luke 23:43) and Paul's words to the Corinthians (2 Cor. 5:8), we are assured His spirit/soul went immediately to heaven; His words to Mary, "I have not yet ascended to My Father" (John 20:17), refer to His yet future physical ascension, not that of His spirit/soul.

Some have appealed to Eph. 4:9–10 and I Pet. 3:19 to try to construct elaborate doctrines to the effect that Jesus spent this time in one way or another in hell. However, this is quite speculative and contrary to historic Christianity. The best view of these passages is that Jesus "descended" to "Abraham's bosom" (Luke 16:22) and declared the home-going day to glory for all who had died in faith, awaiting the coming Messiah-Redeemer.

Read Matthew 28:1–10 and note the following. Who comes to complete the burial process? (v. 1; see Mark 16:1)

When do they come? (v. 1) According to Mark 16:3, what is their concern?

How is the stone moved to allow them access? (v. 2)

Who appears, and what impact does he have on the guards? (vv. 3–4; see Mark 16:5)

What is the reaction of the women to this scene? (v. 5; see Luke 24:4)

What is the angel's explanation to the women? (v. 6; see Luke 24:6–7) His command? (v. 7)

Who intercepts them and with what words? (vv. 9–10)

According to Luke 24:11, what is the disciples' initial reaction to their report? What does Peter do? (Luke 24:12)

According to Mark 16:9–11 and Luke 24:34, who also received an Easter appearance?

WORD WEALTH

Jesus' resurrection is not merely the resuscitation of a dead corpse like that of Lazarus. It is a resurrection to an entirely new dimension of life, that of the age to come. That is, He "dies no more" (Rom. 6:9). This transformed the disciples' outlook, as it gave them "a living hope" (1 Pet. 1:3). That living hope was that of the later resurrection of all believers, who, in Christ, conquer death and the grave forever.

THE GUARDS' REPORT

Matthew alone records the guards' interchange with the chief priests. Earlier the leaders had claimed deceit on Jesus' part (Matt. 27:62–66). Now they practice their own deceit in a desperate attempt to stop the triumph of His resurrection.

Read Matthew 28:11–15. What is the guards' report? (v. 11)

What do the Jewish leaders scheme to do? (vv. 12–13)

Their solution is dangerous and discredits the guards, who could be punished by death for sleeping on duty. This is why the bribe requires a *large* sum of money.

How do they convince the guards to participate? (v. 14)

The soldiers are also comforted because the leaders promise to bribe Pilate if necessary. What is the effect of their scheme? (v. 15)

THE WALK TO EMMAUS

Two unnamed disciples now take center stage during this Easter afternoon. Luke alone reports the details. Mark simply states that "He appeared in another form to two of them as they walked and went into the country" (16:12).

Read Luke 24:13–35 and note the following. What are the two doing when Jesus joins them? (vv. 13–15)

Why don't they recognize Him? (v. 16)

Luke does not specify why they could not recognize Jesus at first. Mark's "He appeared in another form" (16:12) is too ambiguous to lend much insight. Most scholars take "were restrained" (Greek, *ekratounto*) to mean that God had not yet lifted their spiritual blindness (unbelief [see Mark 16:11]) "to enable the disciples to be prepared for the revelation of the risen Jesus by a fresh understanding of the prophecies of his resurrection."[3]

What is their state of mind? (v. 17)

Why is Cleopas surprised at Jesus' question? (vv. 17–18)

How do they describe Jesus? (v. 19) What is their assessment of the recent events in Jerusalem? (vv. 20–24)

"To redeem Israel" is best interpreted in the same vein as similar statements by Zacharias (1:68) and Anna (2:38). The Messiah ushers in the Age to Come, with all its political, social, and ecological transformations. (See "God's Kingdom in the New Testament," chapter 3.)

What is Jesus' response to their perspective? (vv. 25–27)

Even in their grief, Jesus reminds them that things would have been very different for them had they fully accepted what He has been teaching for three years concerning the Old Testament messianic scriptures.

How does Jesus test their attitude toward inviting Him into their home? (vv. 28–29; see Gen. 18:3; 19:2)

What does God do as they eat the evening meal? (vv. 30–31)

"He vanished from their sight" emphasizes the supernatural character of His post-resurrection body.

Though not previously addressed, what was happening within them as they conversed with Jesus along the way? (v. 32)

FINAL POST-RESURRECTION APPEARANCES

During the next forty days, the Synoptics report three additional appearances by Jesus, the third being the Ascension.[4]

Read Luke 24:36–43 and note the following. What is Jesus' concern as He appears to the Ten in an upper room on Easter Sunday evening? (v. 36)

"Peace" (Greek, *eirene*) is to be interpreted against its Old Testament counterpart, *shalom*. It expresses the reconciliation and wholeness available through Jesus (see Acts 10:36). John 20:24 reports that Thomas is not present at this time, but he will see Jesus a week later. Take time to read John 20:24–29, a powerful testimony to the reality of the Resurrection.

What is their response and what is Jesus' concern? (vv. 37–38; see Mark 16:14)

      WORD WEALTH

Troubled, *tarasso*, means "to unsettle, stir up, agitate, disturb, trouble. The word is used in a physical sense (John 5:7), but its primary use in the New Testament is metaphorical. It denotes mental agitation from fear or perplexity (Matt. 2:3; 14:26); an upheaval in the spirit (John 11:33; 13:21); stirring up a crowd (Acts 17:8, 13); confusion resulting from false doctrine (Acts 15:24; Gal. 1:7; 5:10)."[5]

How does Jesus resolve their terror? (vv. 39–40)

How does He further confirm He is "real"? (vv. 41–43)

"They still did not believe for joy" means, "This is too good to be true!"

Read Matthew 28:16–20 and note the following. Where are the disciples now? (v. 16)

What two responses does Jesus' appearance elicit? (v. 17)

What is His "great commission" to them? (vv. 19–20; see Luke 24:44–48)

What is promised to them as they carry it out? (v. 20)

THE ASCENSION

The final post-resurrection appearance in the Synoptics is forty days after the resurrection. It takes place on the slopes of the Mount of Olives, near Bethany.

Read Luke 24:50–53 and note the following. What is His final act toward them? (vv. 50–51; see Acts 1:6–11)

Jesus' final act of blessing is in the tradition of the final blessings of Abraham (Gen. 49) and Moses (Deut. 33), as well as that of the high priest on great feast days (see Num. 6:22–27).

What is their response to His Ascension? (vv. 52–53)

AT A GLANCE

THE APPEARANCES OF THE RISEN CHRIST [6]

Central to Christian faith is the bodily resurrection of Jesus. By recording the resurrection appearances, the New Testament leaves no doubt about this event.

- In or around Jerusalem
  To Mary Magdalene
  (Mark 16:9; John 20:11–18)
  To the other women
  (Matt. 28:8–10)
  To Peter
  (Luke 24:34)
  To ten disciples
  (Luke 24:36–43; John 20:19–25)
  To the Eleven, including Thomas
  (Mark 16:14; John 20:26–29)
  At His ascension
  (Mark 16:19, 20; Luke 24:50–53;
  Acts 1:4–12)

- To the disciples on the Emmaus
  road (Mark 16:12, 13;
  Luke 24:13–35)

- In Galilee
  (Matt. 28:16–20; John 21:1–24)

- To five hundred people
  (1 Cor. 15:6)

- To James and the apostles
  (1 Cor. 15:7)

- To Paul on the road to Damascus
  (Acts 9:1–6; 18:9, 10; 22:1–8; 23:11; 26:12–18; 1 Cor. 15:8)

1. *Spirit-Filled Life Bible* (Nashville: Thomas Nelson, 1991), 1945, "Word Wealth: Jude 11 error."
2. R. T. France, *Tyndale New Testament Commentaries: Matthew* (Grand Rapids: Eerdmans, 1986), 405.
3. I. Howard Marshall, *Commentary on Luke* (Grand Rapids: Eerdmans, 1978), 893.
4. Other post-Resurrection, pre-Ascension appearances are reported in John 20:26–29; 21:1–23 and 1 Cor. 15:5–7.
5. *Spirit-Filled Life Bible*, 1564, "Word Wealth: Luke 24:38 troubled."
6. *Spirit-Filled Life Bible*, 1463, chart on "The Appearances of the Risen Christ."

Writer's Epilogue

We made it! We have walked through crucial aspects of the life and ministry of Jesus Christ from the perspective of three of His biographers. Choosing points of emphasis, scanning other points, and even not mentioning certain truths, was by no means an easy job; as John says, "And there are also many other things that Jesus did, which if they were written one by one, I suppose that even the world itself could not contain the books that would be written" (21:25). I trust that you have personally benefited from the study; I trust that you have been both challenged and stretched in your biblical understanding; I trust you have seen new insights and are endeavoring to practice many of them; I trust Jesus Christ the Son of David . . . the Son of God means more to you than He ever has; I trust this will be but the beginning of a lifelong pursuit of the life of our Lord and Savior, Jesus Christ.

If I would want to leave you with one point emphasized, it would be Jesus' words in Mark 12:30–31, "And you shall love the Lord your God with all your heart, with all your soul, with all your mind, and with all your strength . . . [and] You shall love your neighbor as yourself." As those privileged by grace through faith to be active participants in the kingdom of God because of our being reconciled to God through the work of Christ on the Cross, may we never reduce so great a salvation to easy believism; but may we press on to total commitment and surrender, daily "put[ting] on the new man who is renewed in knowledge according to the image of Him who created him" (Col. 3:10) and daring to believe that "he who believes in Me, the works that I do he will do also; and greater works than these he will do, because I go to My Father" (John 14:12).

May God bless you in your ongoing walk with Him. May His kingdom come; may His will be done, in and through you each day, as we await His coming.